UNITT'S

Canadian Identification & Price Guide to

HOME & COUNTRY
COLLECTABLES

New & Enlarged Edition
with Added Categories

Compiled by
Peter and Barbara Sutton-Smith

D1242352

Fitzhenry & Whiteside

Published in Canada by Fitzhenry & Whiteside, 195 Allstate Parkway, Markham, Ontario L3R 4T8

www.fitzhenry.ca   godwit@fitzhenry.ca

10 9 8 7 6 5 4 3 2 1

Library and Archives Canada Cataloguing in Publication

Sutton-Smith, Peter
        Unitt's price guide to home & country collectables / compiled by Peter Sutton-Smith. — New and enl. ed. with added categories

Includes index.
ISBN 1-55041-858-0

        1. Collectibles—Prices—Canada. 2. Antiques—Prices—Canada.
I. Title. II. Title: Price guide to home & country collectables.

NK1125.U63 2004   745.1'0971'075
C2004-906990-X

Fitzhenry & Whiteside acknowledges with thanks the Canada Council for the Arts, the Government of Canada through the Book Publishing Industry Development Program (BPIDP), and the Ontario Arts Council for their support of our publishing program.

Design by J & S Graphic Design.

Printed in Canada.

CONTENTS

INTRODUCTION

First published in 1992, and reprinted in 1999, this book has become one of the most popular in the much used series of Unitt's Canadian Price Guides.

Not only does it give an insight into the current values of items relating to Home and Country Collectables, but it also gives us a history of things used in the daily lives of our ancestors. Pictured are many of the implements used, which in their day were the "latest" kitchen gadgets, country living and farming aids.

The hundreds of examples come from many sources and are handled by a multitude of different dealers and auctioneers in numerous areas of the country. Thus prices will vary from province to province, and from city to city, according to the prevailing economic climates and the localized costs of doing business.

We thank the many dealers, auctioneers and collectors for their generous help and input, without which this publication would not be nearly as comprehensive.

To Our Readers

May you find the treasure you seek,
Meet old friends and make new ones,
Journey safely and never, never,
sacrifice quality for quantity.

Peter & Barbara Sutton-Smith are the editors of the Canadian Handbook of Pressed Glass and Unitt's Canadian Price Guide to Antiques & Collectables Book 16 & 17, and have been full-time antique dealers for almost 30 years. Both have held the position of Editorial Director of Antique Showcase, Canada's only national antiques magazine, now in its 40th year of publication. Peter also publishes the Antique Showcase Guide to the antique shops of Ontario and is the Vice-President of the Associated Antique Dealers of America.

The Sutton-Smiths are residents of Ontario.

Left: Hires Root Beer dispenser, 1920s.
Maroon lettering on cream pottery ground, silver-plated brass metal pump. Ht. to top of pump 14". Diam. of base 8".
.................................$350-$400

Right: Orange Crush dispenser.
Clear glass embossed reservoir, black glass base with yellow lettering, plated brass spigot. Ht. 13". Base 7" square.
....$250

Cherry Smash.
White porcelain dispenser with gold, red and green decoration. Ht. 15". Diam. of base 8".
....$850

Ward's dispensers, both porcelain.
Left: Ht. 14". Diam. of base 7".
....$450
Right: Ht. 13". Length of base 9".
....$450

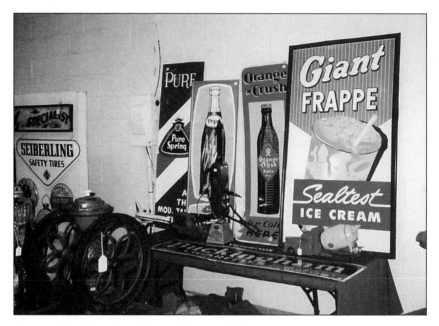

Large advertising signs in excellent condition.

Pure Spring..........**$125**   **Pepsi**...........**$275**   **Orange Crush**...........**$525**

A range of advertising coolers from the 1950s.

BA......................**$185**   **7-Up**...................**$125**   **Coca-Cola**..............**$225**

Red Indian Aviation Motor Oil, *two-sided porcelain advertising sign from 1946.*
....$3,500

French school sign, originally issued by **Coca-Cola** *in the early 1950s. Usually on base with* **Coca-Cola** *advertisement on the back. Similar sign in English shown on base.*
....$500 ea.

(If complete, approx. $2,500)

Wooden prototype for **Mac's Milk** *advertising.*
....$275

Boswell Brewery *(Quebec City) advertising promotion for* **Green Label Ale**, *ca. 1930.*
....$225

American cast iron still bank in the shape of a buffalo, which was an advertising premium used by **Amherst Stores**, *Amherst, New York, ca. 1890.* **$450**

Canadian cast iron stove lifter in the shape of an alligator used as an advertising premium by the **Harrison Stove Company**, *ca. 1880.* **$75**

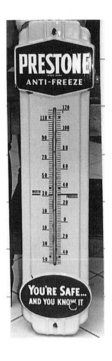 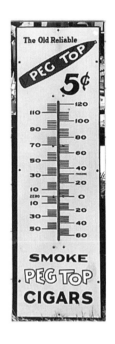 

LEFT:
Prestone Anti-Freeze.
*Red and black on grey
ground, 1940s. Working.*
............................$95

CENTRE:
Peg Top Cigars.
*Yellow on heavy metal
base, 1920s. Ht. 46".*
.........................$325

RIGHT:
7-Up.
*Green bottle, red lettering
on white enamel, late
1950s. Ht. 15".*
...........................$95

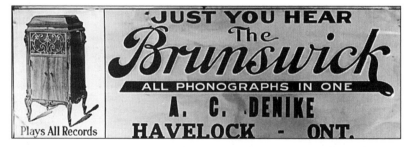

"The Brunswick" *tin advertising sign. Black, white and yellow. Ht. 9½".
Width 28".*
....$235

Clear cut glass wine, etched with the maple leaf and **"Canadian National."** Ht. 5".

.....................................$48

Salt shaker. Miniature replica of **"Ball Perfect Mason"** jar (top missing). Ht. 2¾".

....$45

Medicine measure, tea, dessert and tablespoon measure, **"Jas. Lynch Druggist, Peterborough."** Ht. 2".

....$35

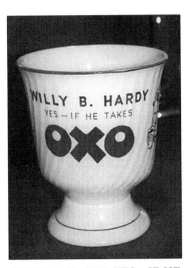

WILLY B. HARDY, YES - IF HE TAKES OXO! English advertising mug.

....$24

Birch bark tobacco box. Ht. 7".
....**$165**

Splint basket, natural and pale green. Ht. 14".
....**$45**

European string basket.
....**$28**

Wicker flower basket. Ht. 10".
....**$22**

Woven basket, buff colour with pink appliqué. Height with handle up 13".
....$48

Woven baskets
Left: Pink and green. Ht. 11".
....$32
Right: Ht. 6¼".
....$16

Two miniature baskets
Left: Ht. 4".
....$15
Right: Ht. 2½".
....$18

Woven basket decorated with applied flowers and bird in nest. Ht. 12".
....$82

Knife box from Ontario. Ht. 23".
....**$125**

Knife box. Ht. 17".
...............................**$185**

Cutlery tray. Pine.
11¼" x 7¼" x 2½".
.........................**$60**

Box, single drawer. Original
red/brown paint. 10¼" x 6¾".
....**$115**

*Document box.
Pine, ca. 1880.
8½" x 9½" x 16".*
...................**$175**

*Document box. Pine, stained
red. 9" x 9¼" x 13¼".*
.....................................**$165**

Sewing box. Diam. 11".
.................................**$130**

*Old order Mennonite pine
cutlery tray from Waterloo
County, Ontario, ca. 1890.*
.....................................**$175**

Victorian walnut trinket/jewellery box inlaid with marquetry and mother-of-pearl. 8½" x 5¾" x 4".
....**$375**

Gentleman's mahogany dresser box, with reverse glass painted hunting scenes, ca. 1890
....**$2,295**

Victorian inlaid mother-of-pearl rosewood box, ca. 1885.
....**$325**

Victorian red leather jewel box with red velvet lining and brass fitments. 12" x 9" x 7".
....**$295**

Austrian cigarette musical box with carved Alpine scene in lid, 1950s. 5½" x 3½" x 2½".
....**$75**

Art Deco cigarette box, ca. 1925. 7" x 4" x 2".
....**$45**

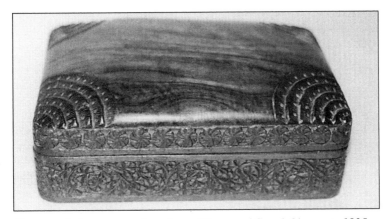

Rosewood cigarette or cigar box with carved floral décor, ca. 1925. 6" x 4" x 2".
....**$175**

*Carved oak letter box.
Ht. 15", width 11¼".
.....................................$225*

*Carved box with concealed lock.
Handle locks lid. Length 8¼".
....$175*

*Tea caddy. Walnut inlaid with
brass and mother-of-pearl.
Length 10", width 5", ht. 5".
....$325*

Dome top storage chest. Pine with iron lock and handles. 33" x 17½" x 17".
....**$225**

Wood and metal humpback trunk, late 1800s.
.....................................**$195**

Mongolian box, mid-19th century.
...................**$1,650**

Small wooden travelling trunk "E. Edwards, GTR (Grand Trunk Railway) No. 42. The Annie MacPherson Home, Stratford, Ontario, Canada."
...........................**$350-$425**
Reputedly over 20,000 children from England came to Canada during the Depression years.

*Sturdy pine dovetailed box.
Length 32", width 20", ht. 19½".*
....**$350**

*Blanket box with initials R.B.
Possibly decorated by a sailor.
Length 36", width 19", ht. 18".*
....**$325**

*Steamer trunk. Pine with metal fittings,
leather strap handles, late 1800s.
Length 34", width 22", ht. 19".*
....**$495**

*Dome top travel trunk/storage
chest, with oak slats and metal
mountings, ca. 1900.
34" x 23" x 19".*
....**$195**

Transitional storage chest. Pine, dovetailed construction, one drawer, lift top to upper storage section, moulded base. 51" x 48" x 22".
....**$575**

Storage chest. One drawer, original cast iron handles, mid-1800s. 28" x 19" x 17".
...................................**$495**

Storage chest. Pine, dovetailed construction. 37" x 20" x 20".
..................................**$275**

Foot locker. Pine, shaped skirt, ca. 1840. 25" x 18" x 18".
............................**$365**

Storage chest. Pine, dovetailed construction, ca. 1860. 27" x 19" x 18¼".
.............................**$345**

Pine blanket box with dovetailed corners, moulded base and original lock, ca. 1840.
43" x 17" x 17".
....**$625**

Dower chest, painted with decorative panels, ca. 1880.
40" x 21" x 19".
.....................................**$695**

An unusual Kentucky blanket chest with carved apron.
....**$13,500**

Pine blanket box/storage chest. Lift top to upper storage area, two drawers with wood pulls, ca. 1850.
....**$325**

Tea Leaf Pattern

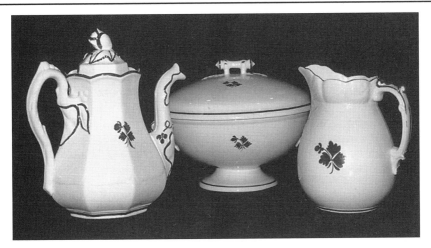

Photos: Courtesy Tea Leaf Club International
Left to Right:
  Shaw Chinese coffee pot $170
  Shaw Footed Cable covered vegetable dish $300
  Wilkinson Maidenhair Fern hot water pitcher $475

Photos: Courtesy Tea Leaf Club International
Left to Right:
  Meakin creamer $195
  Clementson child's creamer $525
  Shaw teapot $400
  Clementson brush vase...$350
  Meakin pitcher..$225

Ceramics - Blue and White

The most commonly found English blue and white china is dinnerware, which was produced in vast quantities during the 19th century. A full dinner service for a wealthy household constituted an imposing array of different plates for soup, the main course and puddings, as well as meat and vegetable dishes, tureens, sauceboats and other items. Side plates for bread and butter were not always included, but there were often twice as many dinner plates as other pieces, which is probably why many have survived.

Such services reflect the extraordinary variety of subject matter that was drawn on for the decoration of transfer-printed wares. The more or less flat surfaces of plates made them particularly suitable for landscape views, and diners appear to have been equally happy to gaze down on Wedgwood's crowded Blue Bamboo pattern or the melancholy romanticism of Ridgeway's Tomb of Kosciuso. In some services each item was decorated with a separate scene or pattern, so that over 50 different engravings could be made for a single service. Others, such as Spode's Blue Italian displayed the same view on each piece. However, the borders on items such as plates were always identical, providing the service with a unifying element.

By the 1830s plate patterns were becoming less dense, and a white undecorated area usually separated the central design from the border. Later in the century a more radical change in fashion undermined the popularity of blue-printed designs, when plates started to be manufactured with brightly coloured borders or left undecorated.

Small platter with extensively pierced rim, ca. 1825.
....$475

*Covered sugar, unidentified
view, maker unknown, ca. 1820.
....$450*

*Davenport platter with a
scene of the Chinoiserie
High Bridge, ca. 1810.
.....................................$650*

*"View of London" with
St. Paul's Cathedral in
the background.
Unmarked, attributed
to Thomas and
Benjamin Godwin.
Overall length 15¼".
...........................$3,500*

The Willow Pattern

The Willow pattern, an English design, was originally derived from the Chinese. Early versions vary a good deal but unless they are marked it is virtually impossible to attribute them to any particular maker. By the first decade of the 19th century a standard pattern emerged which has been used ever since.

It is generally accepted that Thomas Minton engraved the earliest pattern with a willow tree when he was apprenticed to Thomas Turner at the Caughley porcelain factory. He later moved to London where he is said to have engraved copper plates for Josiah Spode. In 1799 he set up in Stoke-on-Trent as a freelance designer and engraver. There can be little doubt that many of the line-engraved designs in the Chinese style which were used by the early Staffordshire makers of blue-printed wares were supplied by Minton. Indeed, several of these early prints are very like designs on Caughley porcelain.

Almost all of the very early versions are either unmarked or marked only with small blue-printed symbols which do not help with attribution. The commonest of these are a small eight-pointed star and a little leaf spray. One early design, despite the fact that it includes a willow tree, is normally called the Two Figures pattern.

The name Willow pattern is now generally applied to a standard design that emerged in the first decade of the 19th century and became very popular in Victorian times. Indeed, it is still produced today. It shows a pagoda with pavilion or tea house on the right, backed by an apple tree. In the centre, a willow tree leans over a three-arched bridge across which three figures are crossing to the left. In the top left, a covered boat crewed by one man floats in front of a small island, and two doves fly in the sky. In the foreground of the design there is a zig-zag fence. There are very many variations on the basic theme.

The Willow Pattern Legend

The standard Willow pattern was extremely popular and legends grew up around the design. These differ considerably in detail but essentially the story concerns a Chinese mandarin, Li-Chi, who lived in a pagoda beneath an apple tree. He had a beautiful daughter, Koong-Shee, who was to marry an elderly merchant named Ta Jin. However, she fell in love with her father's secretary, Chang, who was dismissed when it was discovered that they had been having clandestine meetings. Koong-Shee and Chang then eloped and, helped by the mandarin's gardener, they are seen crossing the bridge that spans the river. The boat is used to approach Chang's house but the furious mandarin discovers their retreat. They are pursued and about to be beaten to death when the Gods take pity on them and turn them into a pair of doves.

A different version of the tale states that the three figures on the bridge are Koong-Shee carrying a distaff, a symbol of virginity, Chang carrying a box of jewels, and Li-Chi, the mandarin, in pursuit with his whip.

Victorian period Staffordshire "Blue Willow" platter in mint condition. 18" wide.
......................................$475

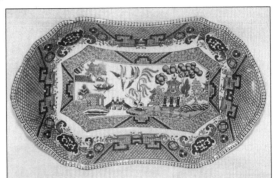

"Blue Willow" relish dish, 8½" wide, semi-vitreous, Buffalo Pottery, 1911.
......................................$75
Note: Relish dishes of this shape were not normally produced by the English potteries.

"Blue Willow" cow creamer, Staffordshire, ca. 1850.
......................................$425

"Blue Willow" transfer ware compote, ca. 1830.
......................................$650

Brown & white platter. "Quebec Harbor & Levis" made for E.T. Thomas, Quebec. Attributed to T. Furnival & Sons, ca. 1870.
....$975

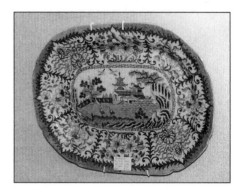

Swansea blue & white platter, 18", "Banana Tree" (sometimes called Chinese Birds), 1800-1810.
....$695

"Maple" pattern earthenware soup tureen, cover, stand and soup ladle, made for the Canadian market by Thomas Furnival & Sons of Staffordshire, ca. 1880. Each piece with brown transfer printed design of a beaver holding a maple branch.
Meat platter
....................................$1,200
Tureen, stand and ladle
....................................$1,500

Plates
................................$275 ea.
Covered sugar
....$450

English blue and white platter, with a scene of the seaport of Madras, ca. 1880.
....**$650**

English open vegetable dish, magenta colour in the Canova pattern, ca. 1860.
......................................**$275**

Platter from an eleven-piece Haviland Limoges fish set, signed L. Martin, ca. 1903.
....**$2,500**

Sauce boat (without stand),
Royal Crown Derby pattern
#3149. Length 7".
......................................$125

Bloor Derby period, hand painted
vegetable tureen, lid with gilt knob,
1811-1848.
....$750

Soup tureen and underplate
from Toulose, France, ca. 1840.
Tureen 15" long by 13" high,
underplate 17½" across.
....$1,395

English gravy boat (without
stand), ca. 1920.
....$45

Soup tureen by Thomas Furnival
& Sons, England. White with
mulberry rim and gold stripe.
Length 12".
....$150

Cauldon Lace pattern soup tureen,
blue on white. Registry mark
under glaze. Length 12", ht. 8".
....$135

Soup tureen, white with gilt trim,
acorn and leaves finial. No maker's
mark. Length 13½", ht. 7½".
....$125

Soup tureen by Brown Westhead
Moore & Co., Cauldon, England.
Blue on white, ca. 1895. Length
13½", ht. 8½".
....$250

Mark on Royal Crown Derby tureen. Dot in circle indicates year made — 1925.

Royal Crown Derby Imari pattern. Sauce tureen with underplate, ca. 1925. Ht. 6½". Diam. of stand 9".
....**$950**

English soup tureen, mid-19th century. Make unknown. Ht. 11".
....**$145**

Covered vegetable dish, English, mid-19th century, with blue flowers on white ground. Maker unknown. Length 12", ht. 5½".
....**$245**

Copeland Late Spode covered vegetable dish with rural scenes and border of hops in blue on white ground. Diam. 11".
....**$275**

*Blue Stoneware Eglinton pitcher.
Impressed, "Published by/William
Ridgeway, Son & Co./Hanley/
September 1, 1840." Ht. 10½".*
....$245

*Blue salt-glazed pitcher. Maker,
Edward Walley, Cobridge, ca. 1845.
Ht. 9".*
....$275

*Terra Cotta pitcher with figures in high
relief. Austrian or German, ca. 1840.
Ht. 10½".*
....$325

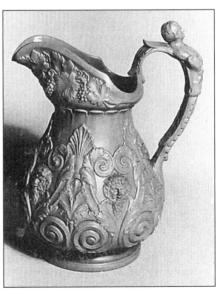

*Biscuit salt-glazed Wedgwood water
pitcher with caryatid handle. Ht. 8½".*
....$375

Green glaze plate, "Grape & Vine with Strawberries," ca. 1895.
....**$115**

Dark biscuit salt-glaze tobacco jar. Ht. 8".
....**$125**

Majolica pitcher, dark green at base to orange/yellow. Decorated with flowers and leaves in relief. Ht. 8¼".
....**$95**

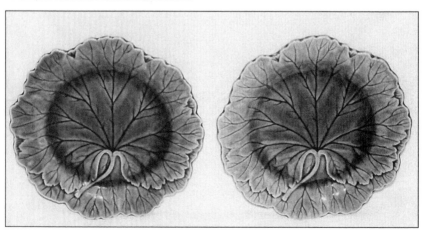

Pair of Wedgwood green glaze plates.
......................................**$85-95 ea.**

One of a set of six hand painted plates decorated with differing fish, blue background and gilded fish shells. Imported from France by Wilhelm & Graff, New York.
....**$1,200 set**

One of four Dresden tea plates. Pink borders with centre décor of swans and bull rushes in relief, ca. 1870.
....**$250 set**

Very attractive "Horse with Foal" plates. Made both by the Poole and Kaiser Potteries.

Small - Poole Pottery
....**$65 ea.**

Medium - Kaiser Pottery
....**$50 ea.**

Large - Kaiser Pottery
....**$65 ea.**

Minton plate, ca. 1810. Chinese influence depicting children riding on a seesaw.
....**$450**

Teapot, "Swiss Pastimes" by T. Hughes & Son Ltd., Longport, England, ca. 1870. Ht. 7".
....$275

Teapot in the form of an Indian tepee, plus the Canadian maple leaf, and inscribed "Greetings from Canada." Clarice Cliff, Newport Pottery, mid-20th century.
....$2,250
(Note: Rarer in Canada than in England)

English "Radford" Rose pottery, 1930s.
Teapot on stand
....$145
Pitcher
....$75

English "Harley" (Lane End, Staffordshire) teapot with swan finial, ca. 1800. (Slight restoration)
....$750

Pair of Wallendorf figures, ca. 1880. 20" high.
....**$3,200**

Staffordshire figure - "The Fishmonger," 19th century.
....**$450**

Staffordshire figure of William III, 1690, ca. 1850. Inscription: "Derry Aughrim Enniskillen and The Boyne."
....**$495**

"Courting couple" mantel shelf figure. Unusual to be decorated all round the back. Staffordshire, England.
....**$345**

Pepper and salt, Mr. Micawber and Sara Gamp, by Beswick, England.
....$95 pr.

Stoneware miniature novelty whisky flask.
....$55

Pepper and salt, baseball players, Anthropomorphic, Japan.
....$35 pr.

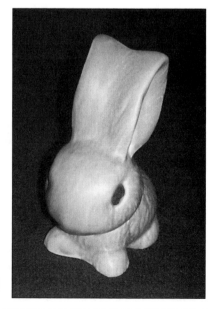

Fawn-coloured extra-large-sized rabbit. Sylvac Pottery, England.
....$195

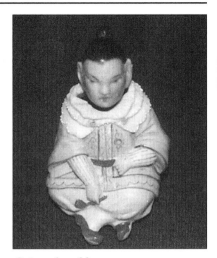

Oriental nodder.
....$125

Turquoise colour Majolica jardinière and stand. Leeds Art Pottery, England, 1880-90. Reg. # 20570.
....................................$1,500

Continental Faience barber's bowl. Late 18th century.
....$875

Pair of French Faience plates from northeastern France, ca. 1880.
........................$375 ea.

Ironstone pitcher in moulded wheat pattern. Stone Chinaware Co., St. Johns, Quebec.
....$275

Cheese dish by F. Fielding, England. Indian pattern, 1882. Typical orange and cobalt colours.
....$225

Delft sardine dish with traditional blue on white decoration and a sardine-shaped finial, ca. 1910.
.....................................$125

Early English blue and white 19th century invalid cup.
...................................$225

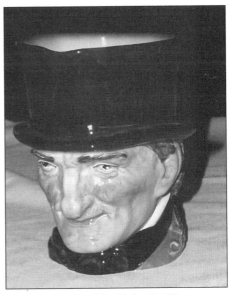

Royal Stanley Jacobean ware with pewter pedestal. English.
....**$325**

"Micawber" character jug by Beswick.
....**$175**

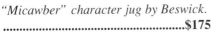

Scenic tile (attributed to Minton). Village scene with church and dovecote within wide oak frame.
....**$165**

A highly collectible "John Peel" character jug by Royal Doulton. Very lifelike with a ruddy complexion, 6" tall.
....**$335**

Dresden figure of a lamb, 19th century.
....$175

"A pair of Horses in action," by Lladro.
Ht. 16".
....$1,600

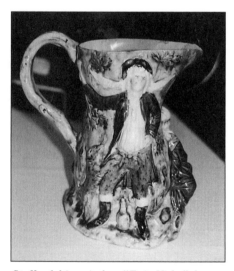

Staffordshire pitcher "Fair Hebe" by
Ralph Wood, ca. 1790.
....$850

Jardinière, white with applied flowers
and gilt decoration. Impressed Moore
(Bros.) Longton, 1868-75.
....$695

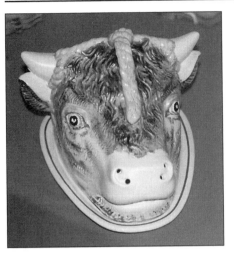

Rare "Bull" cheese dish. English Staffordshire, ca. 1870.
....**$275**

Torquay Pottery Jardinière. Ht. 7". Slip-decorated with coloured scrolls on a green ground. By the Brewer Pottery at Broomhill. A motto inscribed on a cream band over a scroll background is typical of this firm, ca. 1890.
....**$165**

Three glazed Staffordshire pottery fox head and stirrup cups, ca. 1870. Used to serve drinks in at the commencement of the hunt.

Left: Lady's cup. Red fox head with purple grape vine collar. Ht. 4¾".
....**$425**

Centre: Young rider's cup. Red fox head with black collar. Has been repaired. Ht. 3½".
....**$145**

Right: Gentleman's cup. Red fox head with black collar. Ht. 5¼".
....**$450**

Hand-forged yoke, ca. 1850, of Southern
Ontario origins.
....$76

Left: Waterloo County grease bucket from
a Conestoga wagon, ca. 1810.
....$350
Right: Waterloo County wagon jack, dated
1805, perfect working order.
....$425

Canadian pine "creepy" - used as a seat
and holder for nails, when shingling a
roof.
....$125

Rare Indian tobacco cutter, ca.
1860, of the type designed to be
backpacked on trips. It originated
with the Micmac tribe on the Red
Banks Reservation in New
Brunswick. The blade and nails
were all hand-forged.
....$135

Brass blowtorch. Ht. 10". 1920s.
....**$110**

Left: Early pulley, ca. 1880, found on a farm near Bright, Ontario.
....**$75**
Right: Primitive Waterloo County draw knife, ca. 1890.
....**$60**

Ontario Waterloo County pine tool box with strap hinges and original leather strap handle, ca. 1880.
....**$125**

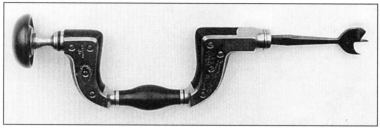

Ebony filled brass brace. Presentation brace: "Ultimatum" made by William Marples, Sheffield, ca. 1860. "Royal Letters Patent by Her Majesty." Length without bit 11".

....**$525**

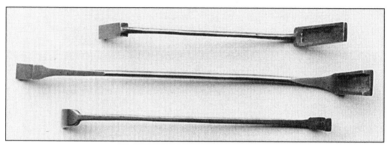

Brass tools, used to make sand moulds for metal castings. Length (center piece) 13".

....**$25 ea.**

Top to Bottom:
Broad axe. Blade width 14".
..................................**$120**
Broad or bench hatchet. Blade width 6½".
..................................**$45**
Broad axe. Blade width 12½".
..................................**$115**
Broad or bench hatchet. Blade width 4".
..................................**$40**
Broad axe. Blade width 13½".
..................................**$110**
Broad axe. Blade width 9¾".
..................................**$112**
Broad or bench hatchet. Blade width 4¾".
..................................**$40**

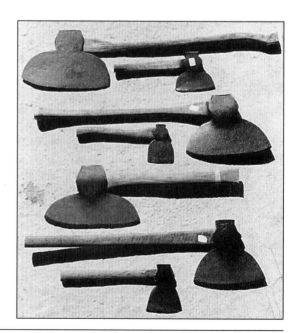

Machine to flatten straw. All wood, pegged construction. Ht. 14". Length of base 13". To flatten straw used in making straw hats and baskets.
....$155

Ice tongs. Length 27".
....$28

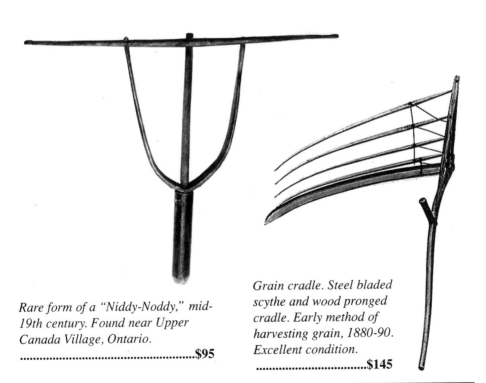

Rare form of a "Niddy-Noddy," mid-19th century. Found near Upper Canada Village, Ontario.
....$95

Grain cradle. Steel bladed scythe and wood pronged cradle. Early method of harvesting grain, 1880-90. Excellent condition.
....................................$145

Saw mill tooth setting hammer. 10-pound head, wooden handle, ca. 1880. Length 10".
....**$85**

Farrier's Butteris. Hoof parer. Hand forged steel, wooden handle, ca. 1850. Length 11".
....**$185**

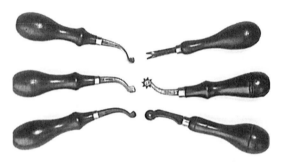

Shoemaker's tools. Steel with brass ferrules, wooden handles. American, ca. 1900. Length 5".
....**$18 ea.**

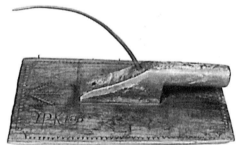

Roof thatching tool. Austrian. Inscribed 1830. Wood base and handle, steel spike. Length 14", width 8".
....**$275**

Hatchel/Hackle. Flax or hemp was drawn through the teeth, separating the coarse and broken pieces of the stalk from the fine fibrous parts. Early 1800s. Length 22".
....**$125**

Nova Scotia butter paddle with heart decoration.
Mid-19th century.
.... **$95**

Maple butter paddle from Riviére-du-Loup,
Quebec, ca. 1870.
....**$55**

Unusual pine spoon made by Mennonites of
Yorktown, Manitoba, ca. 1880. Note the
unique carved handle.
....**$155**

Hand hewn maple butter ladle from Quebec,
ca. 1850.
....**$45**

Mohawk Indian ladle from Brantford area. First quarter 19th century.
....**$235**

Primitive Waterloo County boot jack, ca. 1830.
Used by farmer to remove his boots.
....**$28**

Hand hewn butternut paddle from
Quebec, ca. 1860. Probably used
to remove articles from oven.
....**$45**

Early pine boot jack from western
Ontario, ca. 1820.
....**$32**

Superb English 18th-century skimming spoon carved in elm. Shown
on contemporary bird's eye maple stand.
....**$495**

Plow plane by A. Monty, Roxton Pond, Quebec, ca. 1910. Rosewood body and fence with boxwood wedge, arms and screws and brass fittings.
....**$449**

"Sugar Devil," 1820, most likely American, used to loosen bulk sugar at the general store. Wrought iron with wooden handle. Length 17".
....**$145**

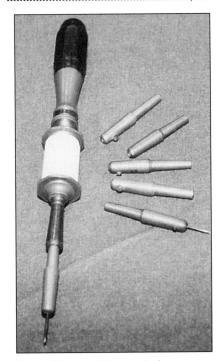

Bow drill with 6 bits made from rosewood, brass and ivory, ca. 1890, by N. Erlandson, N.Y.
....**$500.**
Note: This was a piano maker's tool. In 1870 more New York State households had pianos than bathtubs!

Canadian screw arm plow plane, 1850, beech base with adjustable boxwood threads. Marked "Richard Todd," the name of the original owner.
....**$125**

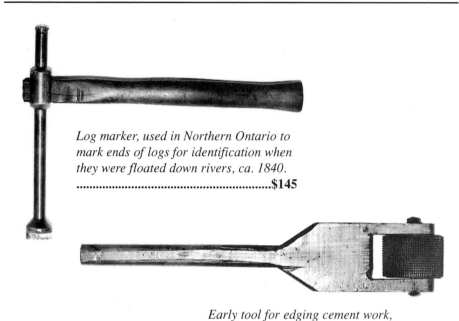

Log marker, used in Northern Ontario to mark ends of logs for identification when they were floated down rivers, ca. 1840.
....**$145**

Early tool for edging cement work, from Quebec, ca. 1890.
....**$125**

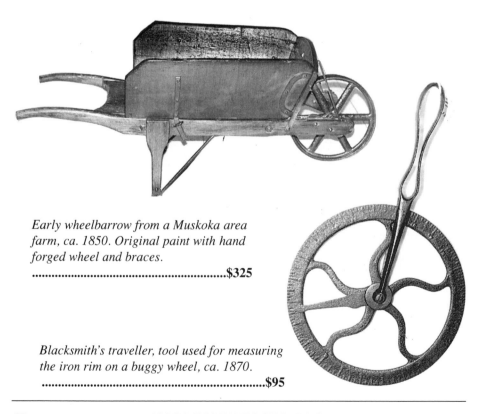

Early wheelbarrow from a Muskoka area farm, ca. 1850. Original paint with hand forged wheel and braces.
....**$325**

Blacksmith's traveller, tool used for measuring the iron rim on a buggy wheel, ca. 1870.
....**$95**

Carpenter's panel raiser plane, 1847-1880, made by Casey & Co., Auburn, New York.
....**$100**

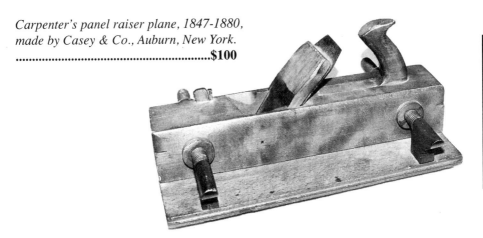

Canadian moulding planes, marked V.A. Edmond 1870-1917. Length 9½".
   Left:
....**$18**
   Right:
....**$18**
Below: Canadian moulding plane with guide. Marked L. Cantin 1850-1889. Length 14".
....**$45**

Scottish mitre plane. Handmade. "Spier's, Ayr," prominent Scottish maker. Dovetailed steel, adjustable blade wedge is brass, rosewood filled back and front. Length 12½".
....**$700-800**

Large steel chisel for smoothing boards. Late 1800s. Length 12".
....$65

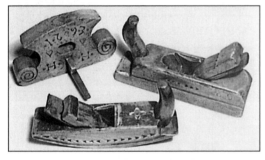

Stanley scrapers. Cast iron frames.
Left: No.12 handle. Length 11".
....$95
Right: No.8 nickel plated.
....$85

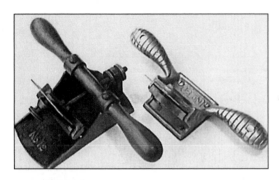

Planes. Austrian.
Left: Inscribed 1793,
H.H. Router. Length 7".
....$195
Right: Inscribed 1869. Stair rail
plane. Length 9".
....$165
Front: Early 1800s. Length 9".
....$150

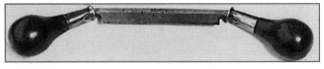

Pattern makers draw knife. Steel with wooden handles.
C.E. Jennings, made in U.S.A. Length 10".
....$68

Logging Tools
Top: Beaver tail. Hand forged. Driven
into floating logs, guide rope threaded
through eye.
....$22
Bottom: Race knife, steel, wood
handle. A scribing tool for marking the
ends of logs. Length 6".
....$58

Antique workbenches nearly always show signs of wear and damage. This one is in wonderful condition. Made of maple and pine, it comes from the Hanover, Ontario area and dates from ca. 1890.
.............................**$2,395**

Maple and pine workbench from Wellington County, Ontario, ca. 1890. 70" x 26½" x 33".
.............................**$2,395**

Shaker's bench, ca. 1840.
...................................**$395**

Work bench, 60" x 27½" x 35" high with cherry top and pine base. Five drawers with brass hardware, ca. 1880, all original.
....$3,200

Pine and maple work bench with oak legs and walnut drawer knobs. From Cambridge, Ontario, all original.
....$2,800

Five bottle cruet. Carousel frame by Meriden "B" Co., with original cut and etched bottles, ca. 1880. Ht. 15½".
....$225

Five bottle cruet. Triple plate carousel frame by Rogers, with original cut and etched bottles, ca. 1880. Ht. 17½".
....$275

Six bottle cruet. Replated silver stand, with cut and etched matching bottles. Ht. 16".
....$295

Silver plate cruet, marked EPNS. No maker's name. Blue and orange pattern glazed pottery, ca. 1890. Ht. 6½".
....$145

Cranberry coin dot pickle
caster in silver plate stand
with tongs.
......................................$325

Cranberry pickle caster with
enamelled decoration in
Meriden "B" Company. Silver
plate stand with tongs.
....$435

LEFT:
*Spinner daisy pickle
caster in Meriden
silver plate stand
with tongs.*
..........................$130

RIGHT:
*Little River pickle
cruet in silver plate
stand with tongs.*
..........................$155

LEFT:
Flower and Quill pickle caster in Toronto Silver Plate Co. stand with tongs.
...........................$225

RIGHT:
Sunk daisy (Cooperative Flint Glass Co., Beaver Falls, Pa.) pickle caster in Meriden silver plate stand with tongs.
..............................$155

Cranberry pickle caster with enamelled floral design in Toronto Silver Plate Co. stand with tongs.
....$435

Cranberry pickle caster with enamelled floral design in Toronto Silver Plate Co. stand. No tongs.
.................................$425

Cranberry pickle caster with enamelled decoration of berries and leaves in silver plate stand with tongs.
....$425

Loop and pillar (United States Glass Company, 1902) pickle caster in Toronto Silver Plate Co. stand with tongs.
.........................$165

Double pickle caster in Toronto Silver Plate Co. stand.
....$275

Jam/Preserve jar, "Illinois" pattern in Meriden silver plate stand with lid and spoon.
....$175

Sugar Shakers
Left: Blue with coin dot.
....$145
Right: "Daisy and Fern," clear with
iridescent. Ht. 5".
....$135

Syrup pitcher, coin spot 9 panel
mould in green opalescent.
....$395

English Tantalus. Oak frame with brass fittings.
Lock and key. Complete with three cut-glass
decanters with original cut stoppers. Length 13",
ht. (to top of handle)12½".
....$325

Vinegar cruet, blue glass with clear handle.
Decorated with butterflies and flowers in
gilt and enamel. Ht. 7¾".
....$145

During the first decade of the 20th century, around 1907, the woven silk and embroidery greeting cards appeared. Each of these types was highly decorative and symbolic in its own way and both justly popular. It is the latter, the embroidery greeting cards, that servicemen on active duty would send home to loved ones. Those with patriotic motifs, like flags, insignia and dates were the most popular and are the ones most favoured by collectors. Those are also the more expensive.

The "date" cards are quite intriguing. Artists often used the colours of our Allies. For instance, this is shown clearly in both the 1917 and 1918 illustrations. Looking at the numbers in 1917, the "1" is embroidered in the colours of the French flag, the "9" in the red, white and blue stars and stripes of the U.S.A., together with the Belgian black, yellow and red colours. The second "1" shows the British Union Jack red, white and blue colours and "7" with the Netherlands red, white and blue across the top, and Italian red, white and green on the tail.

On the other hand, there were those with sentimental words such as "Kind Thoughts," "Happy Birthday," or "To My Mother" (Sister, Brother or other family members). These cards came with pretty, simple designs.

Most of the cards appear to have been produced in France. The actual embroidery was done in bright coloured threads on flimsy material (voile) and the colours usually remain fast on the cards and show little signs of fading even after more than 80 years. In the final stage, the embroidered material is set into a postcard-size frame, sealed and backed. It is then like a regular postcard, ready for the message and address. Those on "Active Service" were allowed to write those words at the top in bold letters and the card was then automatically delivered courtesy of the Armed Forces and the Postal Delivery Service.

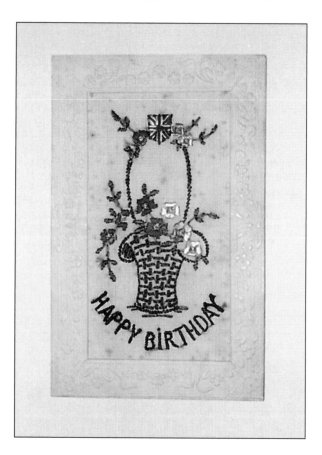

B. S-S.

Cards are to be found in the price range of $15-$25 according to their condition.

Victorian coal scuttle in walnut with elaborate brass fittings.
....**$225**

English brass coal scuttle, complete with shovel and inside metal container. Brass feet.
....**$350**

Brass coal scuttle. Repoussé tavern scene on both sides. Dutch, mid to late 1800s.
....**$350**

Pair of cast iron "owl" andirons (firedogs) complete with their glass eyes. Late 19th century. Ht. 22" **$750**

"If the clothes make the man, the paint makes these owls." Andirons (firedogs) found in Nova Scotia, ca. 1920. ....**$475**

Pair of andirons (firedogs) made at the Saint John Foundry, painted figures depicting Prussian soldiers. Ht. 19". Sold at auction for $310. (Considered well under value for these nostalgic items out of the grand fireplace of the Ashburn Lake Lodge.)

Pair of wrought iron 18th century adjustable firedogs from Quebec, used both for heating and cooking. Food would be placed on rods put into the adjustable (up and down) brackets at the rear of each, and pots utilized the baskets.
.....................................**$2,400 pr.**

Metal wall heating grate. Patented 1871.
....**$325**

"Fish Market" acrylic on board painting by Maud Lewis (1903-1970). 12" x 16".
....$3,500

Model of Royal Canadian Mountie carved in wood by Murray Butcher of Simcoe, Ontario, 1985. Outstanding workmanship finished with real buttons and insignia.
....$7,500

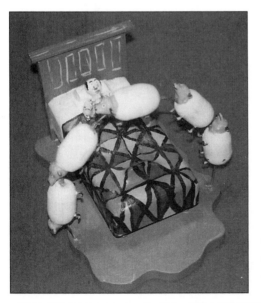

"Counting Sheep" contemporary folk art by Jeffrey Kerras, Prince Edward Island.
....$325

Four folksy bell boys in a row. Found in Whitehorse, Yukon Territory.
......................................$365

Folk art military policeman. Originated from Edmonton.
....$325

Folk art whirligig from Nova Scotia, 1940s.
..............................$195

Folk art, man with sheep dog (on table) by Andre Laporte.
....**$495**

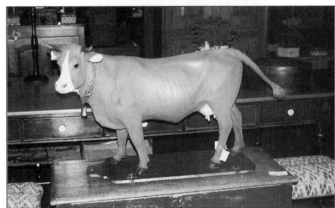

Window display cow from the Eastern Townships.
.....................**$6,100**

Quebec folk art horse and cart (wheels replaced), ca. 1880.
.......................**$2,375**

Oil on wood, Marie Therisa, daughter of Philip IV and wife of Louis XIV. Ca. 1900.
.............................$375

Folk art Santa by Roger Raymond, Quebec.
.............................$475

Pine washstand, ca. 1870, with heavy shell decoration done at later date, originated in New Brunswick, but acquired in Prince Edward Island.
....$995

Three-masted gaff-rigged ship's model with stand and anchor. Overall length 52" x 41" high, beam 9½". Fine attention to detail and rigging.
....$625

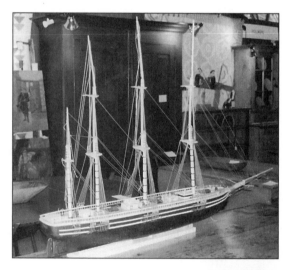

Model of schooner found in Newfoundland. All hand carved with very fine detailing, ca. 1900.
....$1,950

Finely detailed model clipper.
....$350

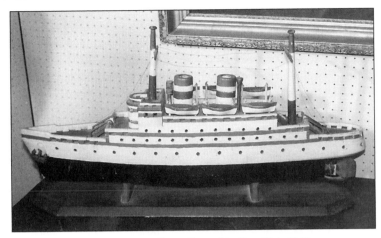

Carved model of an ocean liner. Found in Dunkirk, N.Y.
....**$1,500**

Folk art tole horse, ca. 1920. Found in Eastern Ontario.
......................................**$435**

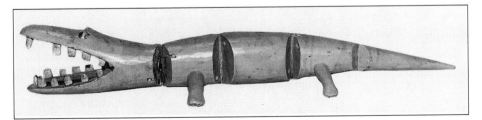

Folk art articulated alligator, from Oxford County, Ontario. Late 19th century.
....**$675**

Noah's Ark with sixteen carved animals and two figures. In original paint. Thought to be of German origin, ca. 1890.
....**$625**

Wooden cutout of jockey on racehorse, from Kitchener area, Ontario.
....**$175**

Indian Folk Art. Elephant carving, ca. 1890.
.........................**$475**

Carved bear from Quebec, ca. 1930.
....$375

Folk Art

Carved Indian from Quebec, ca. 1920.
....$785

Nine pieces from a "John Bull" skittles game. English, 19th century.
......................................$395

Unique folk art sunflower carved cabinet. Early 19th century, Connecticut, U.S.A.
....**$6,900**

Funky pine five-drawer chest from South China, Maine, U.S.A., ca. 1900.
....**$795**
(Wooden water pump, ca. 1890.)
....**$345**

Pine with faux finish, folk art type of chest of drawers, with very unusual handles.
....**$375**
(On top, red painted metal projector.)
....**$65**

Solid pine hanging wall cupboard, ca. 1900, from Lac Megantic in the Eastern Townships of Quebec. Extensive poker art detailing done with a stencil and a hot poker.
....$750

Ukrainian folk art flat-to-wall with all wooden pegs. Late 19th century.
....$1,695

Doukhobor hanging cupboard in pine, early 19th century, from Verigin, Sask.
....$1,250

Oddball folk art hallstand, homemade pine construction. Ash splints and spools used to create decorative top. Note: Attached umbrella and cane stand. From New Brunswick, ca. 1920.
....**$1,205**

Folk art snow goose from Prince Edward Island, ca. 1930.
....**$895**

Folk art cow, with all the important equipment! Contemporary folk art by Jeffrey Kerras, Prince Edward Island. Made from "The Surge Milker," Babson Bros. Co., Chicago, aluminum base, wooden head, leather ears and horns of rebar (used for reinforcing concrete).
....**$495**

Canada goose carved from an old barn beam.
....$325

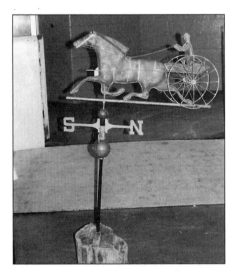

Handmade copper weather vane.
....$1,500

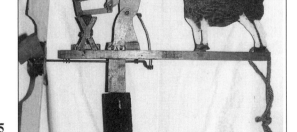

Mennonite whirligig, ca. 1930.
....$395

Folk art carving "Indian & Pony" by Charles Fournier of Lac St. John, Quebec, ca. 1929.
....**$1,850**

Interesting pair of folk art bookends, ca. 1900, with adjustable arms.
....**$550**

Carousel horse, ca. 1890, from "The Carousel of Hemmingford" in Hemmingford, Quebec.
..................................**$4,500**

Folk Art team of horses drawing a sleigh loaded with logs carved by retired harness maker Melvin Bauman of Listowel, Ontario in 1977.
....**$895**

Magazine rack decorated with carvings and poker work. Signed "George Beaver, Alderville, Ont., Can." Mr. Beaver was a well-known Indian craftsman who specialized in this type of work. Ht. 24", width 24".
....**$225**

Folk art sculpture with gesso and paint, ca. 1905.
....**$625**

Folk art fish-shaped cutting board, from New Brunswick, ca. 1920.
....$95

Hand-carved polychrome-decorated fish decoy, by Charles Meloche of Rivière Cunard, near Windsor, Ontario, ca. 1915.
....$190

Quebec "Taverne Art." Anyone who has ever been fishing in the Eastern Townships or the Laurentians, and stopped off for a beer, would be familiar with one of the cousins of this painted wooden fish plaque from the 1960s.
....$75

Folk art birdhouse.
........................**$165**

Handmade birdhouse in the
folk art tradition, ca. 1920.
......................................**$275**

American folk art hand-painted
passenger pigeon on a metal
tray, dating to 1880. Originating
in Syracuse, New York.
....**$325**

American folk art cloth doll, 1910-1920, with the overalls being a marble bag still containing some 25 vintage marbles.
....**$175**

Excellent show towel, in the style of a sampler, from Saskatchewan, dating to the first quarter 20th Century.
....**$375**

Ewald Rentz (1908-1995) was one of Ontario's most celebrated folk artists, mostly known for his prolific creation of distinctive carvings. This large painting is one of a few that he kept as part of his own collection until his death.
....**$3,600**

Whimsical and eye-catching wooden Rentz carving of a woodpecker and blue bird. Overall ht. 21½".
....**$675**

*English spice cabinet,
mid-18th century.*
......................**$1,450**

*Small three-drawer jewellery
chest, ca. 1870.*
......................................**$495**

*Pine sewing box from Quebec in
original paint with hand-forged
nails, ca. 1820.*
....**$695**

i) closed   *ii) open*

Nun's bench and bed. Makes bench when closed, sleeps two when open. From Quebec, ca. 1790.

....**$2,500**

                                                    ii) closed

i) open

Oak smoker's cabinet, with spaces to hold the pipes, the bowls for blending the tobacco and humidor, the container in which the tobacco is kept sealed to keep it fresh. Such cabinets were a man's delight where he could keep all his smoking paraphernalia together. Ca. 1870.

....**$450-$550**

Pine hutch table lift-top seat. Mortice & tenon & dovetail construction. Lancaster County, Ontario, ca. 1810.
....**$4,500**

Unusual carved oak games table with four fold-up shelves, ca. 1920.
....**$550**

Pine apothecary's cabinet.
....**$2,695**

Wooden dental cabinet made by Ransom and Randolph Co., of Toledo, Ohio, U.S.A., ca. 1900.
....$695

Elm wood, sectional filing and index card cabinet.
....$650

Multi-purpose office specialty cabinet in solid quarter-cut oak. Designed to be worked at while standing, the cabinet has four file compartments and several smaller drawers. Ca. 1920.
......................................$975

English oak dental cabinet, ca. 1925. All of the drawer knobs on this piece are different sizes allowing the dentist access to them without looking away from the patient.
....**$1,295**

Pine sideboard, featuring fine panelled doors. Originating in Ontario, ca. 1850.
....................................**$5,250**

Pine buffet, ca. 1870, from Edward County, Ontario.
...............................**$2,965**

Carved oak sideboard, 1920s.
....**$695**

Contemporary pine sideboard with wooden pulls. 80" x 25" x 36" high, natural finish, 2 drawers over 2 doors, a hideaway pull-out serving table containing 2 adjustable centre shelves and shaped apron.
....**$2,500**

English pine sideboard, all original except for feet, ca. 1870.
....**$3,200**

Solid golden oak sideboard with applied floral carved decoration, ca. 1890.
......................................**$2,395**

Pine buffet server from Prince Edward Island, ca. 1870.
......................................**$3,495**

i) closed.

Pine sewing table from Nova Scotia, ca. 1850. Ht. 28½", width 22".
....**$390**

ii) open.

Pine night table with Jacobean style twist legs.
....**$475**
(Brass candle snuffer)
....**$195**

Pine candle table from Nova Scotia. All original. Ht. 28½", width 18½".
....**$450**

Mennonite peg-top table in cherry, from Grey County, Ontario, ca. 1845. Measuring 55" x 33", the top can be released by four pulls for cleaning.
....**$3,895**

This pair of pine lamp tables illustrates how similar styles of furniture appeared in different areas of the nation. To the left is a table originating in the Wilno area, Ontario, ca. 1860, while the table on the right was from Manitoba, ca. 1880. Both priced at
....**$495**

New Brunswick four-drawer mahogany dressing table, ca. 1860. Turned legs, wood pulls, brass casters and shell-carved kneehole. 45" x 23½" x 29" tall, with 8" high carved backsplash.
....**$3,000**

Dressing table. Early 1900s. Two side mirrors missing. Ht. 64", width 33".
....**$650**

Bamboo Oriental-style dressing table. Victorian, ca. 1880. Ht. 65", width 28".
.....................................**$495**

Pine vanity dresser, with original stencilled roses, ca. 1860.
....**$750**

Furniture

Pine chest of drawers with brass pulls, in excellent condition, ca. 1890.
..............................**$1,195**

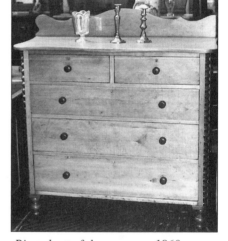

Pine chest of drawers, ca. 1860.
....**$1,200**

Pine bonnet chest from Penetang area, Ontario, ca. 1830.
....**$1,700**

Pine bonnet chest found in Goderich, Ontario. The convex moulding above the bonnet drawers is in fact a secret drawer. Ca. 1850.
....**$1,550**

Basswood & Butternut bonnet chest, Ottawa area, Ontario, 1880-1890.
....**$1,050**
(R.S. Germany cocoa set, pot & six cups & saucers on tray.)
....**$325**

Fine solid oak chest of drawers, probably of European origin, is highlighted by geometric carvings on the outside edges of the drawers and pegged construction clearly visible to the sides.
....**$1,390**

Pine chest of drawers, ca. 1860.
....**$1,345**

Pine bonnet chest with unusual shell carving on centre drawer, from Leeds-Grenville County, Ontario, ca. 1850.
....**$1,950**

Pine miniature chest of drawers. Square nails, wooden pegs and bone escutcheons. Found in Norfolk County, Ontario, ca. 1870.
....**$795**

Miniature pine dresser with white porcelain knobs. From Woodstock area, Ontario.
....**$295**

Miniature chest of drawers, birds' eye maple, flame and burl.
.................................**$850**

Primitive three-legged Waterloo County milking stool, ca. 1860, found in Elmira, Ontario.
...................................**$145**

Unusually small pine step stool, ca. 1870, with square nails. Measures only five by eight inches on top and stands just five inches high.
..............................**$85**

Shaker-style pine foot stool with traces of original paint. From Simcoe County, Ontario, ca. 1875.
.........................**$165**

Washstand - Eastlake style. Walnut with original brass hardware, ca. 1880. Ht. 29", width 30".
....**$750**

Washstand - Eastlake style. Ash, with original teardrop drawer pulls, ca. 1885. Ht. 38½", width 29½".
....**$825**

Washstand - Eastlake style. Walnut with ornately carved back board, ca. 1885. Ht. 38½", width 30" (incl. towel rails).
....**$925**

Washstand - Eastlake style. Pine (primary wood) with original teardrop drawer pulls, ca. 1890. Ht. 42", width 40" (incl. towel rails).
....**$975**

Washstand. Oak and butternut,
ca. 1890. Ht. 32".
....$395

Washstand. Maple from Nova Scotia,
ca. 1860. Ht. 34½", width 22½" (incl.
towel rails).
....$430

Pine washstand, with original
porcelain handles, from
Peterborough County, Ontario.
Early 1800s. Ht. 33½", width 36"
(incl. towel rails).
....$690

Pine washstand in two colours. Height to
top of gallery board 32". Width including
towel rails 26".
....$625

Pine commode with two upper drawers and one lower door, ca. 1875.
....$475

Painted pine commode with back-splash, 24" x 18" x 31" high, single drawer, panelled door and two under shelves.
....$395
On top: Coca-Cola memorabilia, 24 bottle rack, 18½" x 12" x 4½" high.
....$45

Ash commode, ca. 1895.
.................................$450

Pine lift-top commode in the Empire style from Prince Edward Island, with unusual hand dovetailing, ca. 1870.
....$675

Dry sink in original paint. Quebec, ca. 1860.
....$4,500

Rare pail bench cupboard of Polish heritage, in pine with raised panels and scalloped top. From Wilno, Ontario, in original three-colour paint. Ca. 1900.
....$985

Dry sink cupboard in pine and basswood (minor restoration). Marked "St. Jacobs" on back (Ontario). Ca. 1895.
....$6,500

Pine two-piece cupboard, with overpaint removed to original red. Acadian origins.
....$6,995

Pine two-piece hutch, Simcoe County, Ontario, ca. 1865.
....................................$3,500

Pine step back cupboard, original ochre paint. Quebec, ca. 1840.
....$15,900

Pine flat-to-wall cupboard from Omemee, Ontario, ca. 1870.
....$3,295

Two-piece cupboard in poplar. Made in New Jersey, signed and dated 1908 on base.
....$975

European pine one-piece flat-to-wall cupboard, ca. 1875.
....$3,200

Early Wilno cupboard, two-tone cream paint, no restoration.
...................................$18,000

Canadian two-piece corner cupboard in yellow pine. From Hamilton, Ontario.
....$495

Furniture

Golden oak Welsh dresser with five drawers and two small cupboards. Early-mid 19th century.
....**$8,500**

Large pine one-piece flat-to-wall cupboard from Trois-Rivières, Quebec, ca. 1865.
....**$9,800**

Pine armoire, original paint. Quebec, 1870.
...............................**$6,800**

LEFT:
Wilno flat back cupboard with shoefoot Chippendale reedings on corners. Three original colours.
.............**$5,300**

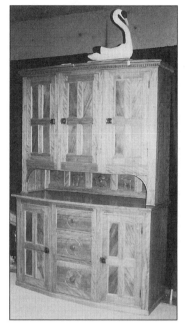

RIGHT:
Flamed birch cupboard, first quarter 20th century from Deschambault, Quebec.
.............**$8,500**

Furniture

Open dish dresser in red over original ochre, single drawer over two bottom doors, with lollipop cutouts on the side.
....................................**$6,200**

18th century open Irish dish dresser.
....**$5,200**

Morris chair, quarter-cut oak
with brass back adjustment.
....$975

Mission oak, late Victorian
rocking chair.
.................................$350

Quarter-cut oak Morris reclining
chair with claw feet and turned
spindles on the side, ca. 1930.
....$1,375

Victorian walnut armchair in the
Jacobean manner, green upholstery,
padded arms and pronounced rope
turning with carved top rail.
48" tall x 22" seat.
....$475

Eastlake Victorian Rocker
together with matching footstool.
.... $475

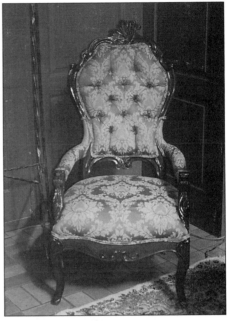

Gentlemen's Victorian chair in
Rosewood. French polished
and re-upholstered. Ca. 1860.
...................................$1,800

BELOW:
A "Knowles" patent sofa with
mechanical drop arms, solid oak
frame, newly upholstered.
....$2,250

Furniture

Nova Scotia Boston rocker. Original paint, curved spindles. Cane seat replaced. Ht. 42½".
....$300

Quebec rocker. Two-piece carved seat, chestnut and pine. Ht. 42".
....$235

Black Boston rocker. Ht. 42".
.....................................$115

Rocking chair. Basswood seat, ash rockers, elm and maple.
....$198

Furniture

Boston rocker with original transfers. One spindle replaced. Ca. 1850. Ht. 40".
....**$420**

Rocker, black with original stenciling. Ca. 1860. Ht. 42".
....**$290**

Oak pressed-back rocking chair with leather seat.
....**$165**

Pine Salem rocker.
.......................**$125**

Nova Scotia Lincoln rocker.
New cane seat. Ht. 43½".
.....................................$295

Rocking chair, butternut and
maple with cane seat and back.
From Bowmanville, Ontario area.
....$275

Walnut nursing rocker with cane
seat and back, plus attractive
partial spindle back.
....$195

Chestnut nursing rocker with
cane seat and back.
.....................................$185

*Nursing rocker. Mixed woods,
ca. 1880.*
.....................................$200

*Boston rocker. One-piece basswood
seat, ca. 1850. Excellent condition.*
.....................................$355

*Pressed back side chair.
Ash and elm.*
...........................$175

*Nursing rocker. Pressed back,
early 1900s.*
.....................................$235

Furniture

Mahogany chair, seat recaned.
Set of six.
..................................$195 ea.

Quebec chair, seat recaned.
Set of four.
.............................$175 ea.

Maple chair, seat recaned.
Set of six.
...............................$195 ea.

Painted Quebec chair, rope-
like woven seat. Ht. 35½".
....$125

Furniture

Ladder back chairs with original stencilling. Rush seats. Ht. 33".
....**$145 ea.**

Pillow back chairs in pine and maple. Set of four.
....**$650**

Canadian arrow back chair
with plank seat, ca. 1825.
.....................................$275

Rare canoe chair, signed "Tubbs
Wallingford, VT."
....$250

Early Swiss marriage chair,
carved with Dolphins, initials
and date.
.....................................$1,600

Oak pressed back commode chair.
Ht. 46".
....$295

LEFT:
Maple hall chair,
ca. 1920.
..................$125

RIGHT:
Oak Windsor chair,
ca. 1850.
...................$2,000

Balloon back dining chairs. Mahogany, early 1800s. Hand-carved with turned legs and fully upholstered red velvet seats. Set of six.
....$2,400

Victorian dining chairs. Late 1800s. Walnut, solid shaped splats, carved crest rails, cabriole legs, drop-in seats. Set of four.
....$1,000

Wooden jardinière set. Metal banded flower barrel with metal insert on wooden stand.
....$350

Mahogany plant stand with splayed supports.
......................................$325
(Brass jardinière)
......................................$250

Victorian pot stand, mahogany veneer. Ht. 38". Diam. (top) 14".
....$275

Cradles

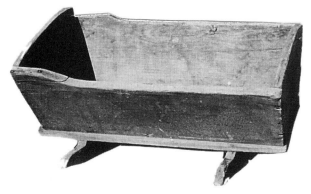

*Primitive pine cradle.
Length 31".*
..............................**$175**

*Quebec cradle. Oak,
ca. 1880. Length 35".*
............................**$155**

*Primitive pine cradle, ca.
1875. Length 22".*
..................................**$110**

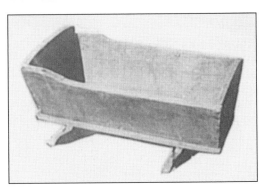

*Pine cradle, ca. 1880.
Length 31".*
.............................**$175**

Furniture

Swinging cradle. Ash with square nails. Quebec, mid-1800s. 36" x 15".
.....................................$450

Victorian cradle. Walnut with spool turning, panelled side and end boards.
.....................................$375

Walnut spool cradle, all original. Length 38".
....$425

Child's Murphy bed of the Victorian period, ca. 1860. From Beauce, Quebec.
...............................$2,450

High chair. Pine with food tray, ca. 1920.
....**$195**

Tiger maple child's dresser
from Ohio, U.S.A., ca. 1840.
...............................**$7,500**

High chair. Ash and pine,
early 19th century. Ht. 31".
...............................**$650**

Child's spool bed. Pine and elm.
Length 53", width 29".
...............................**$475**

Pine Mammy bench rocker, provides
cradle for child and seat for mother.
...............................**$625**

Furniture

LEFT:
Child's chair, maple frame
and rush seat.
.....................................**$270**

RIGHT:
High chair with woven
seat, yellow ochre paint.
Ht. 31".
................................**$335**

Child's press-back chairs. Ht. 24".
Set of four.
....**$350**

Pine child's rocker with cane seat.
....**$145**

Wicker bar stool.
........................$145

Wicker cradle.
.....................$185

Wicker cradle. Carry cot lifts out of stand. Ht. 28", length 31", width 20".
.....................................235

Five-piece wicker patio set, ca. 1910, with newly upholstered cushions.
....**$1,950**

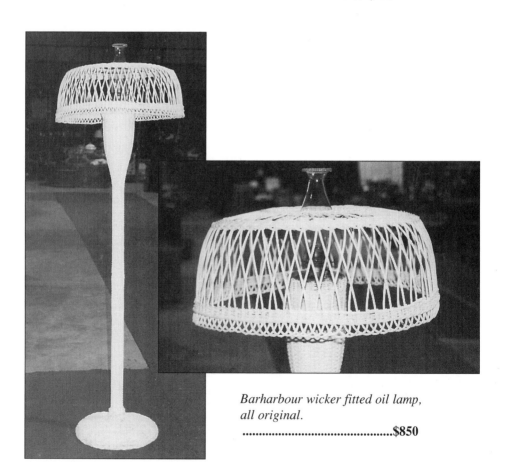

Barharbour wicker fitted oil lamp, all original.
....**$850**

American satin glass fluted shade with painted and gilt leaves and grapes, ca. 1919.
..................................**$75**

American etched glass square shade with inlaid gilt decoration, ca. 1918.
..................................**$62**

Glass

One of a set of six American dark amber glass shades, manufactured by the Jefferson Glass Co., ca. 1919.
..................................**$35**

Cone pattern cased pink sugar caster. Consolidated Lamp and Glass Co., 1894-1904. Ht. 5".
....$145

Clear blown glass cruet, swirl pattern.
....................................$125

Blue opalescent syrup pitcher. Reverse swirl with clear reeded handle. Ht. 7¼".
....$295

Opaque blue glass sugar caster with hand-painted flowers and leaves. Plated top. Ht. 5".
....$325

Extremely rare blue opalescent mould blown Greek Key with Wedding Ring (OMN Double Greek Key) syrup pitcher. Nickel Plate Glass Co., Fostoria, Ohio, and continued as U.S. Glass Company. Ca. 1892.
....$975+

Hand-painted milk glass maple syrup pitcher, ca. 1890. Probably Canadian.
....$135

Coin Dot, blue opalescent syrup pitcher with silver-plated lid.
.................................$275

Glass

Anchor Hocking glass "Moonstone" compote, ca. 1925.
....$295

Silver plate centrepiece with blue opalescent bowl in "Daisy & Fern" pattern.
....$850

Chocolate glass sawtooth mouth covered dish. Manufactured by the Indiana Tumbler and Goblet Company of Greentown, Indiana, ca. 1901.
....$250

These dolphins were originally produced in three variations: "sawtooth mouth," "smooth mouth," and "beaded mouth," and in clear and a variety of colours as well as chocolate and golden and red agate. Original colours include teal blue, cobalt blue, green amber, canary, opaque white, and Nile green. Prices range from $250 for the chocolate sawtooth to $5,500 for the extremely rare Nile green. There are a number of dolphin reproductions.

Milk glass candy
container, Battleship
Maine, Admiral
Dewey's flagship.
Length 7".
.............................$55
(see "Opaque Glass"
by Millard plate 300)

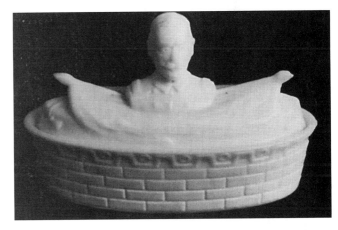

Milk glass candy dish,
Admiral Dewey with
tile base Length 6".
.............................$50
(see "Opaque Glass"
by Millard plate 296)

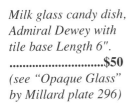

Milk glass hens on
basket. Early 1900s.
Back: 8" long.
.............................$45
Left to Right: 6" long.
...................$37.50 ea.

Vallerystahl milk glass hen-on-nest with tray, six egg cups and covered condiment dish.
....**$400+**

American Hazel Atlas camphor glass salt and pepper shakers, with enamel decoration, ca. 1920.
....**$54**

Circle and fan milk glass condiment stand with salt and pepper shakers, late 1890s to early 1900s.
....**$175**

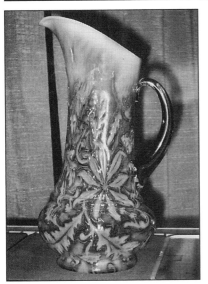

Blue opalescent tall tankard pitcher.
Poinsetta and fern pattern, ca. 1902,
by Northwood, Pennsylvania.
....**$650**

Glass

Rayed heart pattern jam comports
each 5⅜" tall.
Front: Green opalescent
....**$495**
Rear: Blue opalescent
....**$595**

Pressed blue glass 7-piece water set. Early Nugget pattern.
Pitcher height 8¼".
....**$650**

Clear pressed glass plate, "The Queen's Jubilee 1837-1897." Diam. 10¼".
.... $165

Clear pressed glass serving plate produced by the Nova Scotia Glass Co., to commemorate the 50th anniversary of Queen Victoria's reign. Ca. 1887. ....$150

Pressed glass four-piece breakfast set in Beaded Grape pattern, green with gilded rims. NOTE: Gold trim is found on the original items in green glass; reproductions are not decorated in this way. $355

Clear pressed glass Wine, 1910-35. Colonial pattern, Jefferson Glass Company. Ht. 3⅗". **$45**

Glass

Clear pressed glass honey dish, ca. 1870. Lily of the Valley pattern, Boston and Sandwich Glass Co., (or shards have been found at Burlington Glass Works). Ht. 1⅛". Diam. 3½". **$35**

Hazel Atlas Depression glass, apple green. Height of pitcher 6¼".
Pitcher with 4 glasses.
....**$125**

Trento block pattern goblet.
....**$425**

Wildflower pattern goblet, Adams & Co., 1874. USG, 1891. Reproduced L.G. Wright.
......................................**$55**

Westward Ho pattern goblet.
....**$235**

Woodrow pattern. Goblet.
......................................**$175**
Wine.
......................................**$85**

Glass

Flint goblet blown as one piece, solid conica base, ca. 1800.
....$395

Pressed glass etched mug "Lottie," Saratoga, 1894.
....$95

Ale glass, ca. 1880, probably German.
.......................$125

Maple Leaf, opaque blue table set.
....**$1,025**

Milk glass cream jug bearing the
likeness of the Marquis of Lorne.
....**$275**

Cosmos milk glass four-piece breakfast set. Ht. butter 5¾", creamer 7¾".
....**$875**

The bright colourful glass known today as "Carnival Glass" didn't start out life with that name - that came much later. The iridized press-moulded glassware was a process originated in 1907 by Frank Fenton of the Fenton Art Glass Co. in Ohio. It was an immediate success and gave them a head start in making and marketing the new wares. In a short time iridized ware was being produced by other U.S. companies, followed by England, Australia and other countries. Each vied strenuously with its competitors to capture a strong foothold in the market.

Through the following years this type of glassware was produced in great quantities with a variety of shapes and patterns. Housewives loved the coloured glassware; it was affordable and attractive and useful. They also saw it as an alternative to the glamorous but much more expensive Tiffany iridescent types.

The iridescence which is characteristic of this glass was applied by spraying the surface with a chemical substance before firing. This resulted in a satiny finish, which accented highlights across the surface, rather like oil on water effect.

Of the many colours used, marigold is far the most common. Certain colours, however, are rare and consequently far more costly. Red or ice blue, for example, and if combined with a rare pattern, the cost can jump in some instances to four figures. However, new colours and those combined with edge treatments, together with patterns, long based on naturalistic motifs, were issued up to 1930. With unemployment and the Depression its popularity plummeted.

It was then that the massive stocks held in warehouses were sold off cheaply to bazaars or to companies to use as premiums or prizes by fairs and carnivals. Hence the ware became stuck with the name "Carnival Glass."

Although the ware is now reproduced, interest in the old carnival glass has gained many collectors. For those wishing to know more on the subject and its over 1000 patterns there are several good books available.

B.S-S.

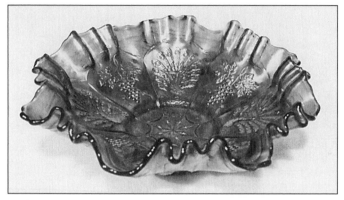

Carnival glass bowl, peacock and grapes pattern in amethyst by Fenton Glass Co. Diam. 8¾".
....$200

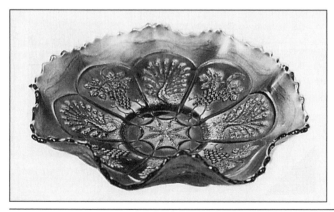

Carnival footed glass bowl, butterfly and berry pattern in amethyst/purple by Fenton Glass Co. Ht. 3¾". Diam. 10".
....$225

Carnival glass bowl, peacock and grapes pattern in amethyst by Fenton Glass Co. Diam. 8½".
............................$200

Carnival glass punch set, a fashion design in marigold by Imperial Glass Co., in the 1950s. This is a very popular pattern in the geometric field. The large bowl rests on a separate stand and there are six matching cups, which usually hang from the side on wire hooks. The entire set is 10¼" in height and is 10½" across the bowl. $295

Pair of Carnival glass vases, prism and diamond design in marigold by Davidson's of Gateshead, England. ....$65 pr.

Carnival glass tumbler. Butterfly and berry pattern in cobalt blue by Fenton Glass Co. Ht. 4". $125

Glass

Carnival glass bowl, orange tree pattern in green by Fenton Glass Co. Diam. 12".
.....................................$175

Carnival glass bowl, Persian medallions pattern in amethyst/purple by Fenton Glass Co. The bowl is covered with medallions straight from the world of Islam with the top edge casually ruffled. Diam. 8¾".
.....................................$155

Carnival glass bowl, holly pattern in marigold by Fenton Glass Co., 7½" deep.
....$65

Carnival glass bowl, vintage pattern in green by Fenton Glass Co. Diam. 8½".
.....................................$70

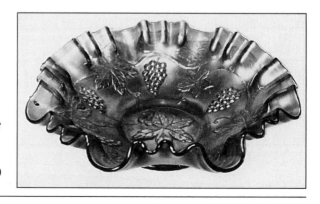

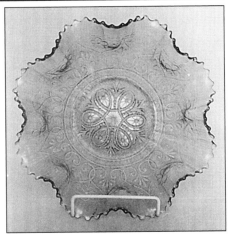

Carnival glass bowl, hearts and flowers pattern in ice blue. Diam. 8½".
....$475
A very are intricate, delicate and pretty pattern. Some pieces carry the "N" for Northwood mark. It comes in most of the usual carnival colours.

Carnival glass vase. Beaded bull's eye in marigold by Imperial Glass Co. Ht. 10".
....$65

Carnival glass vase, ripple threads pattern in marigold by Imperial Glass Co. Ht. 8¾".
.....................$40

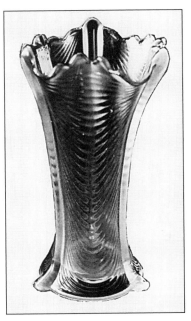

Carnival glass vase, drapery pattern in iridescent blue by Northwood Glass Co. Ht. 7".
....$325

Glass

Doulton jardinière, "Jackdaw of
Rheims," ca. 1890.
....$1,200

Roseville pedestal jardinière
and stand., in the Peony
pattern, a late line introduced
in 1942. One of the more
affordable Roseville offerings.
....................................$1,150

Miniature Nippon jardinière. Cobalt
blue with gold trim and "Toronto,
1907." Ht. 4".
....$125

Weller Pottery jardinière. (See Huxford's
Encyclopedia of Weller Pottery)
....$250

Comos milk glass breakfast set.
(page 132)

Early copper seperator.
(page 169)

English banquet lamp.
(page 183)

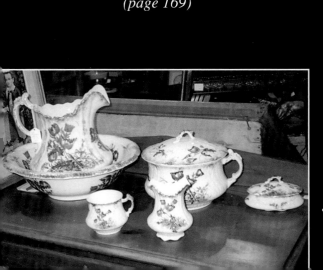

Jug and Basin set. Hilda pattern.
(page 300)

Quebec Pine steb back cupboard.
(page 100)

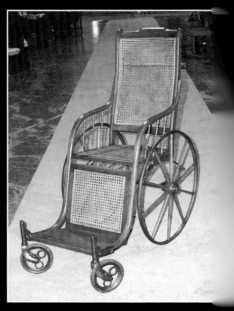

Oak wheelchair.
(page 293)

Victorian cc scuttle.
(page 61)

Wheelbarrow type grain scale.
(page 231)

Early Wilno cupboard.
(page 101)

English pine sideboard.
(page 87)

Cherry and pine work bench.
(page 52)

Sharp Brewer's stone jar
(page248)

**Metal Charlie
Chaplin figure.**
(page 191)

1911 Coronation souvenir tin.
(page 266)

**Mamod Model
steam wagon.**
(page 285)

**Canada Straight
cigarette tobacco tin.**
(page 263)

Copeland - late Spode 1897 Diamond Jubilee Teapot.
(page 250)

Minton Plate.
(page 31)

German grey Stoneware jug.
(page 251)

Miniature chest of drawers.
(page 94)

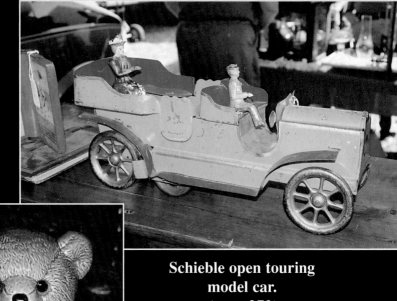

Schieble open touring
model car.
(page 273)

"President's Choice"
cookie jar.
(page 148)

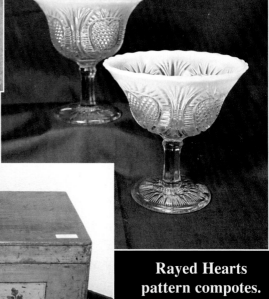

Rayed Hearts
pattern compotes.
(page 127)

Mongolian
box.
(page 15)

1926 C.W. Parker Carousel horse.
(page 298)

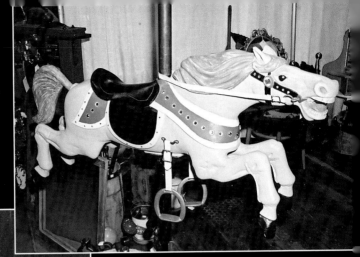

Folk art carving by Ewald Rentz.
(page 81)

"Fish Market" by Maud Lewis.
(page 64)

Ontario hooked rug.
(page 215)

Quebec folk art.
(page 66)

Quebec hooked rug.
(page 220)

Terra Cotta Ware jardinière with enamel decoration. Ht. 5"
....$250

Staffordshire jardinière by Grimwade. Red carnations on blue ground. Ht. 8½".
....$85

Staffordshire jardinière, "Langley Ware," Lovatt Langley Mill, England. Blue top, grey background, ca. 1895. Ht. 6".
....$275

Hadley Worcester jardinière with ram's head handles and peacock decorated panel by W. Powell, ca. 1908.
....$6,500

Satsuma ceremonial jardinière, ca 1860.
....**$525**

Chinese blue and white jardinière.
....**$485**

Doulton Burslem jardinière with attractive floral decoration, ca. 1895.
....**$475**

Doulton Lambeth Stoneware jardinière, 1891-1910. Ht. 8½".
....**$850**

Knife cleaner invented and patented by Spong & Co., in 1880. Oak wooden circular drum mounted on cast iron stand. Solid brass fitments.
....**$395**

Patented Knife Cleaner

With present day modern kitchens filled with the most up-to-date gadgetry designed to make the preparation of our food and drink, or to make every conceivable cleaning task relatively easy, it is difficult today to imagine how much drudgery went into those same household chores just one hundred years ago.

A Regular Chore

Cleaning table silver and steel cutlery (knives) for instance, was once a regular weekly household chore. Careful preparation of the cleaning paste had to be undertaken before the task of cleaning silver could even begin.

The steel cutlery easily stained, and to remove these unsightly spots frequent scouring with strong common washing soda was required - disastrous on the hands - then polished on a buff leather or India rubber mounted on a board. Knives, best kept warm and dry, were most commonly stored in a cutlery box hung near the fireplace in order to prevent rust marks appearing.

The Servant's Friend

Imagine the relief felt by many a kitchen or scullery maid when the knife cleaner was invented and patented by Spong & Co. in 1880. In its original advertisement it read: "The Servants Friend; Patent Knife Cleaner," and it went on to further claim that "The Servants Friend does not belie its name, quickly imparting a lustrous polish to the knives."

The cleaner consisted of a large wooden drum mounted on cast iron legs. Grooves, surrounded by solid brass, were spaced along the top of the drum into which the knife blades were inserted. A handle fitted to the center of the drum turned an inner wheel fitted with leather leaves; these combined with emery powder cleaned the blades. Four to eight knives could be cleaned at a time, taking about a minute to complete.

Good Shiny Results

By the end of the 19th century, several different cheaper kinds of knife polishers were on the market. From this we deduce that they were a popular kitchen "aid" giving good shiny results. The knife cleaner illustrated has an inner wheel fitted with brushes. These work on the same principle as the leather leaves.

Above: Cake pan. Hand punched tin with strap handles. Probably used to "sugar top" a cake with a decorative motif. Mid-1800s. Diam. 9". Ht. 4½".
....**$65**

Right: Cake decorator. Tin with brass connector. Originally came with several types of tubes. Ca. 1910. Length 7".
....**$22**

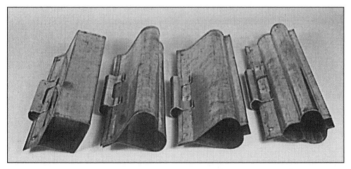

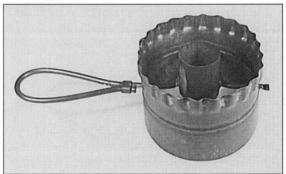

Above: Ice box cookie moulds. Diamond, heart, spade and club. 1920s. Length 9". Set.
....**$35**

Right: Cookie donut cutter. Tin. Could also be used as a funnel. Ca. 1910. Diam. 3".
....**$18**

Cookie cutter. Tin, stamped "Think of Five Roses Flour." Strap handle. Early 1900s. Ht. 1¼".
....$18

"Tart King, Patents Pending" tin tart crimper. Possibly British, early 1900s. Diam. 3".
....$20

Left: Tin flour dredger. Fills from base. Ca . 1900.
....$18
Right: Powdered sugar shaker. Tin. Ca. 1900. Ht. 4".
....$15

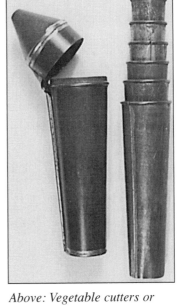

Above: Vegetable cutters or corers. In tin box with hinged lid. Three or four cutters missing. Ca. 1870. Box ht. 6½".
....$35
Left: Percolator funnel. Tin, for use with cloth filter. Ca. 1910. Length 6". Diam. 3".
....$18

Tin Moustache cup. Mid-1800s. Ht. 4¼".
....**$65**

Travel warming vessel. For use on small spirit or kerosene heater. Tin, hinged lid, handle folds into pot. Late 1800s. Ht. 7".
....**$48**

Above: Jelly jars. Twist close tin lids. 1920s. Ht. 3½".
....**$10 ea.**
Left: Quart milk/cream can. Tin, strap handle on lid. Mid-1800s.
....**$40**

Jelly moulds. Tin lids. Early 1900s.
Left & Right: Round with fruit pattern base.
............................**$12 ea.**
Centre: Oval. Length 3". Ht. 2".
............................**$12**

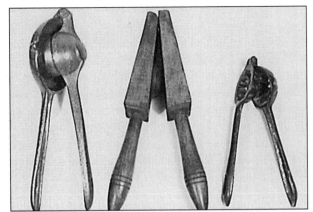

Juice Extractors
Left to Right:
Cast iron, orange juicer.
Late 1800s. Length 10½."
......................................$35
Wood, lemon juicer. Mid-
1800s. Length 11".
......................................$65
Cast iron, lemon juicer.
Late 1800s.
......................................$28

Ladle. Tin bowl, black
wood handle. Late 1800s.
Length 15".
..................................$35

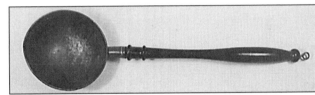

Ladle. Wood bowl,
black handle. Early
1900s. Length 14".
............................$35

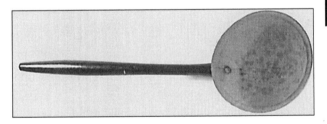

Fish Slice. Perforated
tin with black wood
handle. Late 1800s.
............................$55

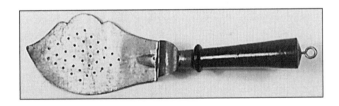

Mixing Spoon. Slotted
tin with black wood
handle. Patent date
March 30, 1903.
..............................$25

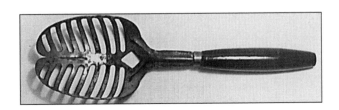

"Old McDonald Farm" spice jars, depicting boy, girl, horse, turkey, Ma and Pa.

....$425

Cream mixer.
....$60
Ice bucket with tongs.
....$44
"Windmills" pattern by Hazel Atlas, 1930s.

10-piece kitchen canister set. German ceramics decorated in the Dutch style.

....$275

Nut meat choppers, both embossed "D" in diamond on base.
Left: Red metal hopper and lid. Ht. 6".

....$20

Right: Red metal top and removable cap. Ht. 5¼".

....$18

Continental 14-piece kitchen condiment set.
....**$245**

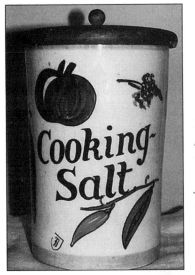

This early 1960s hand-painted jar by the English potter, Toni Raymond, has a distinctive mark on the base, depicting a goose in flight. The wooden lid is attached by a rubber seal for air-tight freshness. Storage jars became less imaginative in design from the mid-1960s onwards. By the 1980s, reproductions of early designs were popular.
....**$35**

3-piece ceramic container set. Made in Italy, 1950s.
.......................**$125**

"Teddy Bear" ceramic cookie jar. Ht. 11", unmarked.
....$35

President's Choice ceramic promotional cookie jar. Ht. 11½".
....$48

Harker Pottery Co. Petit point pattern on cream ground. Rolling pin may be filled with water. Length 15".
....$125

Harker Pottery Co. Petit point pattern on cream ground, silver trim on handle and rim. Creamer, ht. 4".
......................................$22
Milk pitcher, ht. 6".
......................................$40

Harker Pottery Co. Petit point pattern on cream ground. Serving spoon, length 9".
....$18
Custard Cup, ht. 2".
....$8

Porcelain rolling pins, advertising Ogilvie's Royal Household Flour.
....................................$495
Wooden moulds rolling pin.
....................................$395

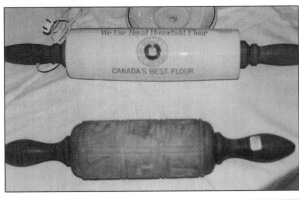

"Swankyswigs" appeared on the market during the Depression. The name applies only to glasses that contained cheese spreads manufactured and packed by the Kraft Food Company. Several "Swankyswig" patterns were made for Kraft by the Dominion Glass Company in Canada. Those made exclusively for the Canadian market are marked on the base with a "C." Information on styles, colours and series is given in "Swankyswig, A Pattern Guide and Check List" by Ian Warner.

Kiddie Kup, red. Tulip No.3, red. Bustlin Betsy, blue. 3¼" high.
....**$10 ea.**

Forget-me-not, red. Posy pattern, jonquil. Tulip No.1., black. 3¼" high.
....**$10 ea.**

Swankyswigs
Left: Posy pattern, Cornflower
No.2, dark blue. Ht. 3³⁄₁₆".
....$10
Right: Band pattern No.2,
black/red/black. Ht. 3⅜".
....$10

Right: Tom & Jerry punch bowl with six mugs, red
coaching scene, green lettering and quaffers.
....$245

Forest green diagonal
ridged pattern glass
containers with aluminum
lids. Late 1940s.
Cereal. Ht. 7¼".
...................................$35
Shakers (with spaces for
labels). Ht. 4¼".
............................$18 ea.
Flour. Ht. 7¼".
...................................$35

Beater, green glass bowl. Marked "Vidrio Products Corpn. Chicago." Ht. 10¾".
....$55

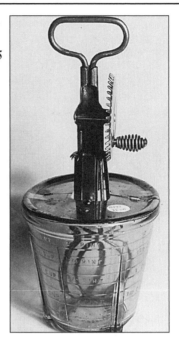

Depression glass, Refrigerator storage set, amber. Large dish 8" x 8". Medium dish 4" x 8". Small dishes 4"x 4". Set
....$75

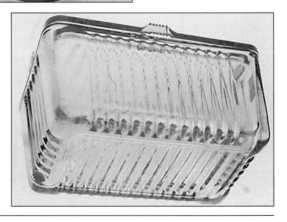

Depression glass measuring cups with graduated measure. Both green. Ht. 4¼".
Left:
.................................$50
Right:
................................$56

Depression glass butter keeper, pink. 5" x 3" x 3".
....$55

Rum cask, ceramic, gold and pink on white ground, brass tap. Possibly Minton, ca. 1870. Mint condition with original top. Ht. 13".
....**$435**

Figural bottle, barmaid in green dress. "Williams & Humbert Sherry." Possibly Wade, ca. 1950s. Ht. 6½".
....**$135**

Parian game pie dish, relief decoration of game on top and sides, ca. 1830. Marked Thomas Fell. Length 11".
....**$750**

Blue Willow pattern, white enamel teapot.
....$125

Blue graniteware stacking dinner pail, four sections plus heating base, ca. 1920.
....$350

Enameled tin teapot with painted scene of Niagara Falls.
....$190

Graniteware merchant's platter decorated with a painted beaver and maple leaf decoration. From Aylmer, Quebec, ca. 1850.
.............................$395

Pearl-grey Graniteware scoop. Length 7".
....$40

Graniteware pitcher with tin lid and carrying handle. Height, handle up 14".
....$35

Pearl-Gray Graniteware measures
Back, Left: "Sheet Metal Products Co. Ltd." ½ gal.
....$50
Back, Right: "General Steelwares Ltd." 1 qt.
....$40
Front, Left: ½ pint.
....$50
Front, Right: "Thomas Davidson Mfg. Co. Ltd." 1 pint.
....$40

"Pearl" washboard by Canadian Woodenware Co., Winnipeg, St. Catharines & Montreal. Glass scrubbing surface. 16" x 8½".
.........................$35

"Economy" washboard by Canadian Woodenware Co. Glass scrubbing surface. 24" x 12".
....................................$25

Copper boiler, late 1800s. Wood grips on handles. 26" x 14" x 12".
..................................$175

Candle mould, tin, 18 tubes. 1800s. 15" x 10" x 10½".
....................................$195

Tin candle moulds.
Height 11".
Six tube
...............................$95
Four tube (not shown).
...............................$65

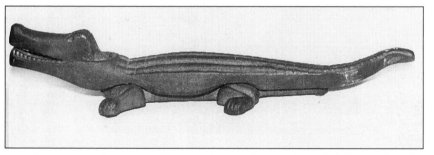

Cast iron nut cracker, ca. 1900, possibly manufactured at a St. Thomas foundry.
....$75

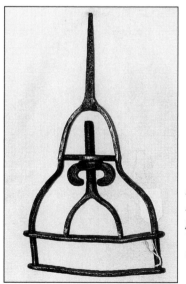

RIGHT:
Gridiron dating
from around
1810.
....................$300

LEFT:
Hand-forged
primitive mop head,
Waterloo County,
Ontario, ca. 1860.
...........................$155

Butter moulds, late 1800s. Swan, 3½". ....$75 Cow, 4". $80

Georgian copper crust crimper. $45

Pie funnel, early 1900s, black lettering on white glazed pottery. $32

Oval tin mould with wheat sheaf design, 4½" x 6". $65

Copper kettle. Ht. to top of handle 12½".
....**$175**

Copper kettle. Ht. to top of handle 9".
....**$145**

English copper water jug, ca. 1860. Ht. 15".
....**$225**

Copper kettle. Ht. to top of handle 8".
....**$155**

Canadian kettle, "McClary's Model Pat. 1903. Made in Canada." Original nickel plating on copper. Six quart size.
....**$175**

Coffee mill, No.2, by Archibald Kendrick & Sons, West Bromwich, England. Pat. No. 608, 1874. Ht. 12½".
....$425

Cast iron coffee mill made in England. Ht. 6½".
....$165

Coffee mill, tin and brass. Top slides open to receive beans. No maker's name, ca. 1920. Ht. 8".
....$130

Coffee mills of home size were first made about 1890. The larger ones made for stores and restaurants often bear a much earlier patent.

Wooden coffee mill, early 1900s. Ht. 9½".
....$125

Coffee mill, twist-off base. Japanned bronze colour cast iron. Latest patent date, June 11, 1878. Ht. 6". Base 4½" square.
....$135

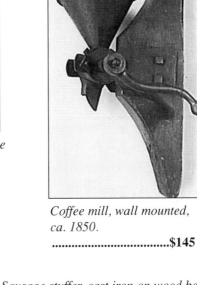

Coffee mill, wall mounted, ca. 1850.
.....................................$145

Sausage stuffer, cast iron on wood base, early 1900s. Length 14½".
....$110

Fruit/Vegetable press, tin, wood presser, 1920s. Ht. 9".
.....................................$45

Mortar & pestle. Cast iron pestle has wood handle. Ht. of mortar 8".
....$145

Apple peeler, cast iron gears and frame, wood handle (blade missing). Length 10".
..............................$90

Cast iron raison seeder, "Wet the Raison," by the Enterprise Mfg. Co., Philadelphia, Pa., U.S.A.
....$55

Apple peeler, mfd. by The C.E. Hudson Co., Leominster, Mass, U.S.A. Patented Jan. 24, '82.
....$65

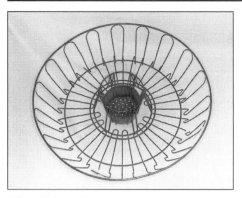

Wire dish strainer.
...........................$55

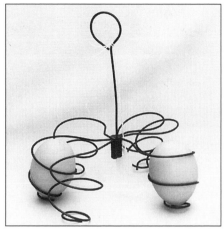

Wireware egg rack.
...........................$48

Wireware pie rack.
....$75
Pie fork with wooden handle.
....$18

*Adjustable pot strainer,
late Victorian.*
.............................$125

Dough box on stand, mid-1800s. Butternut, pine and basswood. 30" x 18" x 26".
....$575

Wooden juice press from Shanghai, 14" long by 6" wide. Late 1800s.
....$140

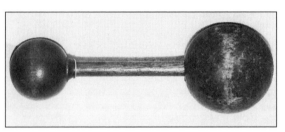

Treen Ontario sock darner, mid-19th century.
....$38

Canadian origin salt box, original finish, ca. 1900.
....................................$85

Pine dough box, ca. 1870. Ht. 11". Width 15". Length 26".
....$265

Pine dough box. Ht. 31". Width 15". Length 26".
....$325

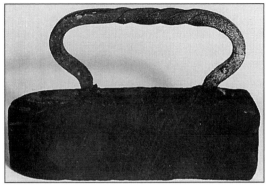

Tailors' goose (poor condition). Length 10".
....$18

Tailors' goose, cast iron, 16 lb. Length 10".
...................................$38

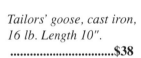

Coleman gasoline iron. Length 10".
................................$65

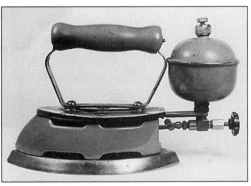

Coleman gasoline iron, "Model 4-A Instant Lite." Turquoise body handle and font. Length 11".
...................................$90

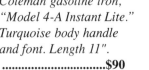

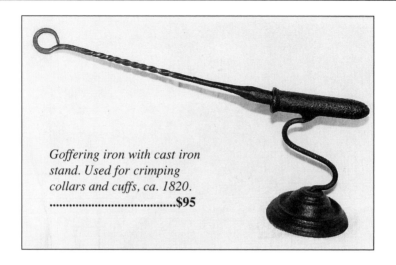

Goffering iron with cast iron stand. Used for crimping collars and cuffs, ca. 1820. ....$95

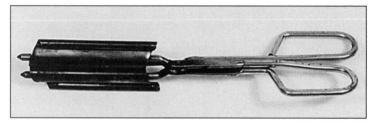

Hair curling iron, double. Length 8¾". $25

Sad iron No.2, Taylor Forbes, Guelph, Ontario. Double pointed, original handle. Length 7". $35

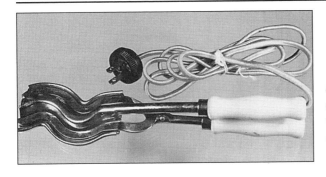

"The Natural" electric curler. Patent pending, ca. 1930. Nickel plated, white enamel wood handles. Length 10".
.................................$35

Travel curling iron. Steel folding iron with ivory handles. Brass spirit heater, folding stand, ca. 1900. Length 10".
...............................$125

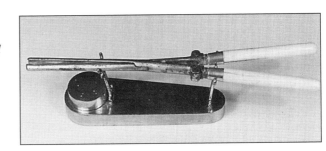

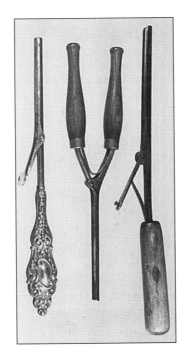

Moustache curlers
Left to Right:
Sterling handle
.......................$35
Wood handle
.......................$18
Wood handle.
Length 7".
.......................$12

Shaving stand, nickel plated with opaque glass bowl. All original. Ht. 15½".
...................................$125

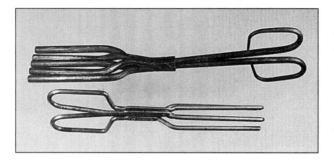

Early hair curlers
Above: Hand forged
steel, double waver, late
1800s. Length 12".
...................................**$40**
Below: Nickel plated
curling iron, early 1900s.
Length 8".
...................................**$12**

Folding curling tongs
Above: Steel tongs, wood
handles. Length 8".
...................................**$12**
Below: Steel tongs, black
wood handles. Length 6".
...........................**$17.50**

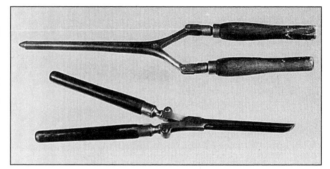

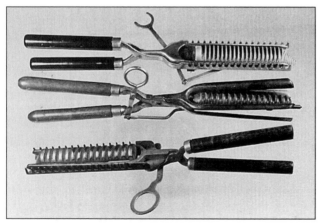

Ringlet curlers
Above: Electric by
Marcelwaver Ltd.,
London, Canada. Patent
date Feb. 3, 1920. Cord
not shown. Length 12".
...................................**$75**
Below: No maker known.
...........................**$55 ea.**

Unusual brass trivet on bun feet. Decorative gallery with diamond cut-outs and iron base with heart cut-out.
....**$275**

Early copper separator.
..............................**$145**

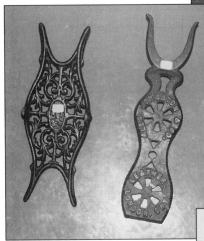

Boot scrapers
Left: Brown Bros, Chicago, unusual reversible.
....**$295**
Right: Alex Johnston & Co., Leather, London, Ontario. Figural stylized beetle, ca. 1870.
....**$595**

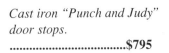

Cast iron "Punch and Judy" door stops.
....................................**$795**

Pine washing machine and
wringer, Beatty Bros. Ltd.,
"Red Star," Fergus, Ontario.
....$625

2nd floor pump made in
Brockville, Ontario. As advertised
in Eaton's 1941 Catalogue.
....................................$200-$250

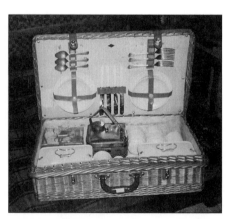

Wicker picnic basket complete with
contents for 4 persons, including square
copper kettle on spirit burner made by
Ilat, 1920-30.
....$145

Reverse swing arm electric toaster,
made by Torrid, Hartford,
Connecticut, U.S.A., ca. 1920.
....$75

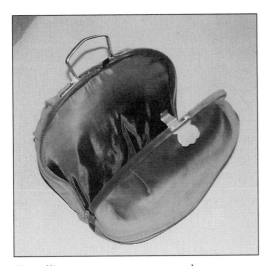

*Travelling teapot cozy, orange velvet
with red silk lining.*
....**\$65**

*19th century wooden washboard,
originally stained green, from Quebec.
The board is 1⅜" thick, 27¾" long and
12" wide, with 23 horizontal slats.*
....**\$125**

*Wicker basket with tea kit,
consisting of spirit lamp,
kettle, tea caddy, small flask
and match box. 19th century.
Ht. with lid closed 8½".*
......................................**\$165**

Close-up of bread drawer.

Kitchen cabinet, oak with agate glass, complete with original latches, flour sifter and bread drawer. Label reads "Sellers kitchen cabinet, the best servant in your home. Southampton, Ontario." Work top, porcelain glazed by the Pittsburgh Patent Glass Company, ca. 1940.
....$1,650

Pine and elm size baking table, made in Manitoba, shown open and closed.
....$850
On top: Yellow ware bowl "Turkey droppings."
....$165
Large Robinson Ramsbottom bowl in dark cream with brown band.
....$275
Cream/blue small covered crock.
....$48
Brass shoeshine stand, ca. 1890.
....$80

"Chatham" kitchen cabinet.
..................................**$2,850**

Two section kitchen cabinet, early 1900s, with original hardware and glass. By Manson and Campbell of Chatham, Ontario (stamped on back).
....**$1,895**

American bake table/cupboard, of ash, maple and pine. Sugar and flour bins in lower section with hutch top. 72" x 44" x 24".
....**$1,275**

Late-1800s oak ice box with exceptional detailing.
..................................**$1,395**

Mid-20th century plywood panelled ice box with metal lining and chrome racks.
...........................**$250-$275**

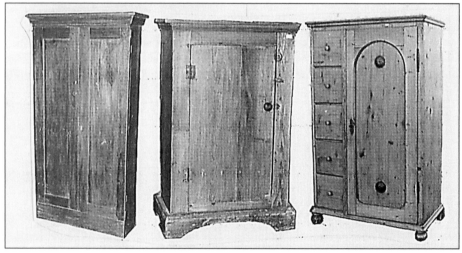

Left to Right:
Preserve cupboard, pine, from Fenelon Falls, Ontario, ca. 1850. Five shelves, peg and tenon construction. 60" x 30" x 9½".
....**$750**
Pie or jelly cupboard, pine, three shelves, from Quebec, ca. 1840. 50" x 33" x 16".
....**$575**
Larder. Ventilated bread and pie cupboard with drawers for flour and spices, etc. European, stripped pine. 66" x 40" x 22".
....**$1,750**

Base of St. Lawrence hand lamp.

St. Lawrence hand lamp. Other name:
Hudson-Como. Ht. to top of collar 3½".
Left: Apple green, applied handle.
....**$365**
Right: Mediterranean blue, applied handle.
....**$435**

Little Buttercup lamps. Ht. to top of collar 3".
Left: Blue, applied handle, original burner.
....**$275**
Centre: Clear, applied handle, original burner.
....**$100**
Right: Amethyst, applied handle.
....**$275**

Guardian Angel lamps. Embossed "L'Ange Gardien Extra - C.H. Blinks & Co., Montreal."
Left: Amber, applied handle. All original. Ht. to top of shade 6¾".

....**$895**

Centre: Electric blue, applied handle.

....**$895**

Right: Clear, applied handle, green shade.

....**$630**

Nutmeg lamps. Brass handles. Ht. to top of collar 2½".
Left to Right:
Green. **$215**
Opal. **$190**
Clear. **$95**
Blue. **$215**

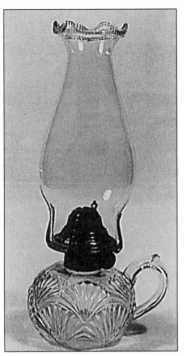

Erin fan. Green. Ht. to top of collar 9¾".
....$320

Clustered fans. Clear. Ht. to top of collar 3".
....$140

Fan. Clear. Ht. to top of collar 10¼".
....$165

Stand lamp. Similar to Zipper Loop. Suncast. Ht. to top of collar 10¾".
....$130

Bullseye stand lamps. Green.
Left to Right:
Ht. to top of collar 7½".
......................................**$258**
Ht. to top of collar 9".
......................................**$286**
Ht. to top of collar 10".
......................................**$330**

Bullseye flat hand lamp. Clear.
Ht. to top of collar 3½".
....**$275**

Bullseye footed hand lamp. Green.
Ht. to top of collar 5½".
....**$250**

Chain with star. Electric blue, applied handle. Ht. to top of collar 4".
......................................**$415**

Cable. Emerald green. Ht. to top of collar 3".
....**$380**

Princess feather. Cobalt blue, applied handle. Ht. to top of collar 3½".
....................................**$435**

Ten panel. Electric blue, applied handle. Ht. to top of collar 2¾".
..............................**$195**

Frosted butterfly. Clear. Ht. to top of collar 11¾".
....$545

Canadian drape. Clear. Ht. to top of collar 11".
....$470

Squirrel. Clear. Ht. to top of collar 7½".
....$495

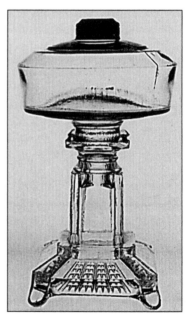

Gesner. Clear. Ht. to top of collar 8½".
....$415

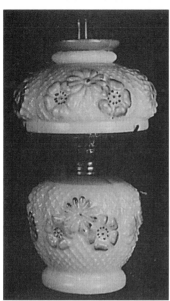

LEFT:
Opaque white Cosmos lamp and shade, with blue shading on shade and font. Ht. to top of chimney 8½".
.......................**$525**

RIGHT:
Sitzendorf parlour lamp. Font held by three cupids, decorated in pink, green and yellow applied decoration. Ht. to top of collar 6".
.......................**$1,135**

Left to Right:
Flat Hand Lamp. Overlay of end-of-day swirl on white, applied handle. Ht. to top of collar 4".
....**$225**
Markham Swirl. Flat hand lamp. Clear with opalescent and clam broth, applied handle. Ht. to top of collar 3½".
....**$495**
Sheldon Swirl. Opalescent and cranberry font on brass base and stem. Ht. to top of collar 5".
....**$425**

Hanging hall lamp with swirled ruby glass shade on an ornate brass frame. Patent date 1876.
....$1,350

Hanging lamp with cranberry shade, jewelled frame and coloured prisms. Patent date 1880.
....$2,950

Brass student lamp, dated October 28, 1879. Clearly marked as a salesmen's sample, original salmon coloured shade and clear glass chimney.
....$2,500

Pink satin glass banquet lamp with double burner. The silver plate base depicts the English Rose, the Scottish Thistle, the Irish Shamrock and three Griffins.
...................$2,100

LEFT:
American opaline miniature lamp with milk glass chimney and gold banding decoration. Patent dates of April 13, 1875 and March 21, 1876 on the collar.
...........................$185-$200

RIGHT:
English Bristol glass miniature lamp. The base is opalescent painted with a floral design, and the chimney is milk glass. It has a typical English brass collar and burner and dates around 1880.
......................$175-$225

English banquet lamp with cranberry glass font and brass Corinthian column on ebonized base. Original shade with cranberry flashed rim and acid-etched floral design, ca. 1890.
.................$2,250

English pew lamp. Brass with ornate cranberry shade.
......................................$1,375

Miniature oil lamps were originally used as "night lights," often holding only just enough oil to burn through the night. Many manufacturers advertised them as such.

Oil lamp with unusual flowered globes, dated 1890.

....**$750**

Majolica pottery lamp with figural handles, ca. 1890. Attributed to Germany, 17" tall with a Hinks burner. Inscribed on the thumbwheel, "No.2/Hinks/Lever." (See "Oil Lamps #2" by Catherine Thuro).

....**$1,695**

English satin glass diamond quilted table lamp with enamel and gilt decoration. Twist type font fitment (prior to screw). Attributed to Webb or Stevens & Williams, ca. 1880.
....**$4,500**

American cranberry glass lamp with chimney. Bull's eye variant pattern.
...............................**$325**

Rosenthal early 20th century perfume lamp in form of an owl.
...............................**$475**

Lighting rod ball, pale amber,
"Shinn-System."
....$65

Lighting rod ball, suncast
amethyst, "Elecrtra."
...................................$55

WEATHER VANE ARROWS - *opposite page, above.*
Stamped zinc horse, embossed with an "E" in a
diamond. Cast iron arrow. Length 22".
....$750
Cast iron arrow. Cobalt blue insert. Length 18".
....$350

KITE-TAILED WEATHER VANE ARROWS
- *opposite page, centre.*
Pebbled green glass insert.
....$300
Pebbled purple glass insert. Length 22".
....$375
"Hawkeye" pebbled yellow glass insert.
....$450

WEATHER VANE ARROWS - *opposite page, below.*
"Snowflake," cast iron with acid-etched flash ruby
glass insert. Length 18".
....$375
Cast iron acid-etched flash ruby glass insert.
Length 18".
....$525
"Fleur-de-lis," cast iron with acid-etched flash
ruby glass insert. Length 18".
....$350

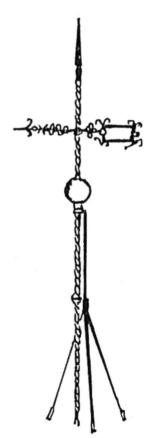

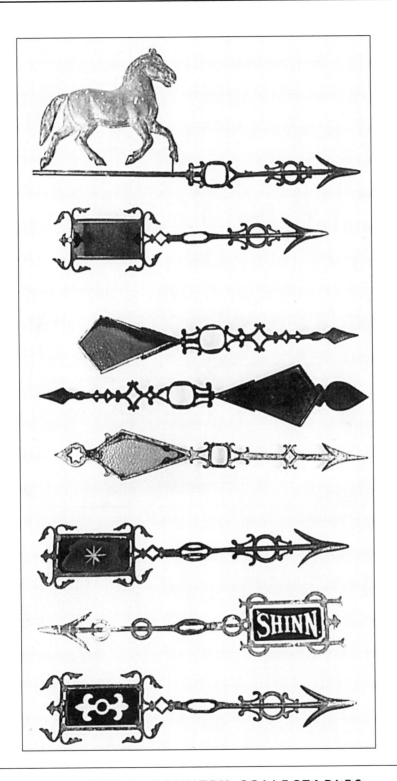

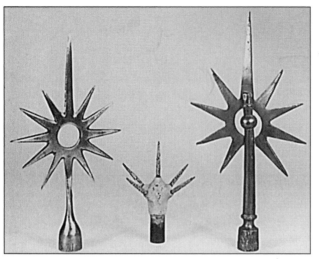

LIGHTING ROD POINTS
Left to Right:
"Crown Point," brass,
maker unknown.
.................................$65
"Sattelite Tip," copper,
corroded to green. Maker
unknown.
.................................$45
"Crown Point," brass, by
Cole Brothers Lightning
Rod Co.
.................................$65

Lighting rod ball, silver mercury,
"Pat'd July '78."
...$225

Lighting rod ball, silver mercury,
"Shinn-Belted."
...$195

Milk glass lighting rod balls:
"Ribbed Horizontal."
....$45
"Plain Round." Diam. 3½".
....$36
"Diddie Blitzen."
....$54
"Doorknob."
....$30

"Baseball," milk glass.
....$75
"Staircase," white porcelain.
....$60
"Mast," milk glass.
....$105

Glass balls and weather vanes added character and a certain charm to the functional rod and strip of the lightning protector. Most barns had two lightning rods - maybe just as well - so one at least might survive the target practice!

Weather vanes have been around for hundreds of years, but the glass balls were a North American innovation, manufactured from around the 1860s to the 1960s. Historically interesting, weather vanes have been prized as decorator items for a number of years and the balls are sought by glass collectors. Exposure to the elements and vandalism have contributed to scarcity.

Cast iron rooster signed E.M.H. 1867. Attributed to E.M. Hummer who was noted for his creative weather vane weights.
....**$225**

Metal "Charlie Chaplin," by Austin Productions Inc., 1972. Ht. 14".
....**$130**

An early 19th century carved wood, and iron decorated stock.
....**$2,500**
You know how they punished people in the town square? They put their heads and arms in a stock!

Stoneware garden gnome. These were popular garden ornaments in the 1920s. Ht. 22".
....**$375**

1. *Bear trap, double spring. Length 46".*
....................................**$425**
2. *Bear trap, double spring. Length 36".*
....................................**$425**
3. *Muskrat trap. Length 14".*
....................................**$45**
4. *Wolf trap. Length 10".*
....................................**$135**
5. *Bear trap, single spring. Length 20".*
....................................**$295**
6. *Fox trap. Length 20".*
....................................**$125**

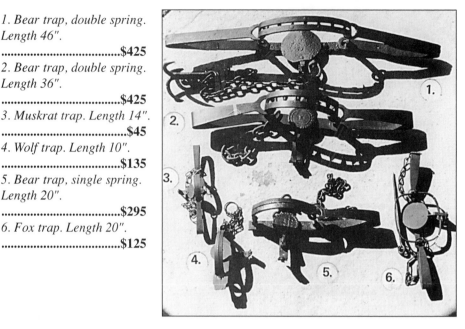

The Cadillac of chicken coops. Pine, 7' x 29". Mid-1800s. Note the protruding dividers to prevent chickens from pecking each other. For use as a kitchen/bar working top with storage under.
....................................**$3,400**

Quebec green and black
miniature safe or bank.
......................................$395

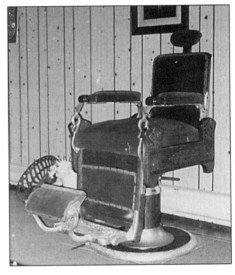

Barber's chair. Upholstery and
mechanism in good condition.
....$695

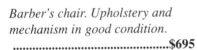

19th century telescopic surveyor's
compass, signed W & LE Gurley,
Troy, New York. With original
dovetailed wood box.
....$925
In the foreground: a 19th century
surveyor's compass, signed W &
LE Gurley, Troy, New York. With
leather case, signed Hughes
Owens Co.
....$400

Personal printing press, ca. 1870. The People's Printing Press by Royal Letters Patent, manufactured and sold by D.G. Berri, 36 High Holborn, London. Dated Feb. 1871.
....**$450**

Stevengraph "Peeping Tom" dated 1862.
....**$225**

Cod salt scoop, pine front with birch back, from Nova Scotia.
....**$195**

Combination bamboo walking stick and parasol.

....**$45**

Decorative copper powder flasks with measuring caps. The design on the sides of the powder flasks is usually made by stamping the metal into a mould. The shell pattern is quite similar to shells found on carved furniture. Early 19th century.

....**$125 ea.**

Miscellaneous

Bakelite radios:
Left: FADA Bullet.

....**$7,500**

Right: Addison.

....**$4,400**

*19th century "Family Tree,"
beautifully lithographed with
ornate detailing and portrait
cameos, ca. 1870.*
....**$140**

*Solid brass French door lock,
manufactured by Penn Hardware,
Reading, Pennsylvania.*
....**$275.**

*Cuspidor (spittoon). Blue enamel on metal with decorative gilding, ca. 1900.
Detachable cover. Ht. 5". Width 12½".*
....**$35**

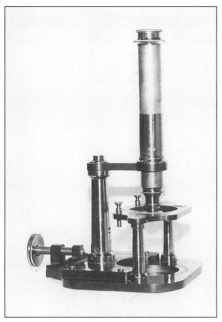

Irish origin Victorian lacquered governess collar and cuff box, ca. 1885.
....**$195**

Miscellaneous

Scottish "Lizars" textile microscope, ca. 1890. Including original handwritten instructions signed by J. Lizars.
....**$850.**

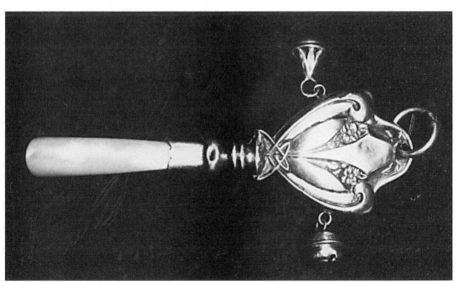

English sterling baby rattle with mother-of-pearl handle, hallmarked Chester 1840.
....**$325**

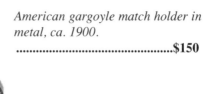

American gargoyle match holder in metal, ca. 1900.
....**$150**

Cast iron still bank in the shape of a two-story bank building. Probably American, ca. 1880.
....**$275**

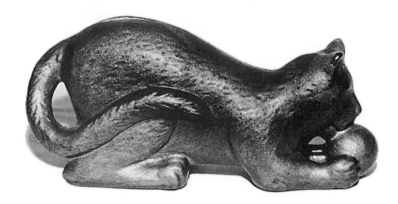

American cast iron still bank in the form of a cat with ball, ca. 1905.
....**$250**

American cast iron Indian and canoe, ca. 1905.
....**$295**

American double burner "Magic Lantern" projector by L. J. Marcy, patent date 1866-69. The lens signed "Darlot," Paris, France.
....**$450**

Walnut Bell Organ & Piano Co., Guelph, Ontario, 6 octave, 2 sets of reeds, plus gallery top, ca. 1900.
..................................**$950**

Walnut Sherlock Manning Co., 6 octave, 2 sets of reeds, 2 couplers.
..................................**$750**
(Organ stool).
..................................**$155**

LEFT:
Organ stool, by the
Dominion Organ &
Piano Company. Oak,
early 20th century.
........................**$145**

RIGHT:
Organ stool, with
ebony finish and
padded seat.
...................**$165**

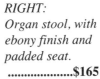

Musical

LEFT:
Organ stool, walnut
with cast iron legs and
original horsehair seat.
.............................**$175**

Organ/piano stool
with metal feet.
..........................**$150**

Organ/piano stool, by the Thomas
Organ Company. Maple with
metal and glass claw ball feet.
....**$175**

Gramophones

The earliest mechanical music was made by the tower clocks of Europe, with figures appearing and striking bells. Since that time music made by machines has taken many forms using bellows, rollers and other devices. The invention of the phonograph by Edison in the late 1800s heralded the great era of popular recorded music.

Canadian Berliner's gramophone. Known as the "trade mark" machine. Made in Montreal, pat'd. Feb.24, 1897. Base 10" square, ht. of horn 16".
....$1,700
Victor dog, plastic reproduction, ht. 18".
....$75

Gem roller or cob organ, with four rollers. Stencil decorated ebonized case, dated 1857. 18" x 12" x 15".
....$800

Concert Gem roller organ, with five cobs or rollers, ca. 1860. Bellows operate when crank is turned. Case 18" x 12" x 15".
....$1,500

Olympia disc music box, from a tavern in Stratford, Ont. Coin operated, uses small Canadian nickels, ca. 1883. Hand carved mahogany case with painting inside lid. With 12 discs. 26" x 14" x 24".
....$6,500

Thorens disc music box. Inlaid basswood case, ca. 1933. With 12 discs. 17" x 13" x 8".
....$2,500

Musical

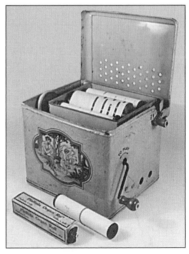

Dutch book organ. Plays music from slotted pages in book, which sits on left bracket and is fed over machine to right bracket. Bellows and pump organ operated by crank. Ebonized case with ceramic and hand painted decorations, ca. 1880. 21" x 11" x 14".
....$2,500

American PlaRola organ, by PlaRola Corp., Easton Md., ca. 1924. Yellow litho tin box. Operated by bellows, 2 cranks, play and rewind. 3 paper rolls. 7" x 7½" x 6".
....$200

Peter Pan box camera gramophone. American, early 1920s. Crank wind and speed control. Length assembled (left) 16". Leatherette case closed (right) 6" x 5" x 7".
....**$300**

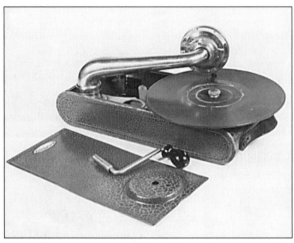

Peter Pan gramophone. American, early 1920s. Collapsible metal horn, crank with speed control. Leatherette case 6" x 4" x 6".
...............................**$275**

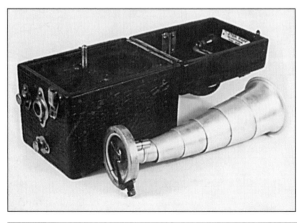

Thoren's "folding camera" gramophone. Swiss, mid-1920s, in leatherette case 11" x 5" x 2". Mint.
.............................**$450**

Symphonion disc player. Magnificent player with 40 discs. Heavily carved walnut case with gallery and finials, ca. 1880. All original. Ht. 7'6". Width 33". Depth 20".
....$17,500

Symphonion disc music box/clock. German, ca. 1900. Disc music box played at the hour or as an alarm. 30-hour clock, walnut case. 12" x 7" x 7".
....$1,800

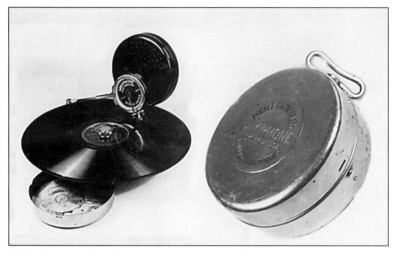

Mikiphone pocket phonograph. Swiss, ca. 1924, plays 10" 78 rpm records. Horn is made from two-piece celluloid inner case. Nickel plated case, diam. 4½". $350

Group of record player needle boxes. Prices vary according to rarity. ....$8-$75

Edison "Home" model
with cygnet horn, ca.
1907. Oak case with
cover. Ht. to top of
horn 41".
.............................$895

Ceramic dog. American, ca. 1950.
Ht. 6½".
....$35

Salt & pepper, promotion, came with
purchase of Victor machine, 1920s.
Ht. 3".
....$45 pr.

Plaster dog, ca. 1920, has Victor
impressed on front. Ht. 4".
....$60

Original His Master's Voice dog,
ca. 1920. Ht. 15".
....$175

Metal dog bank with flock finish,
ca. 1918. Ht. 6½".
....$225

Victor V phonograph, with handmade
mahogany base and horn, ca. 1907.
Base 14" x 14" x 8".
....$2,500

Duplex Phonograph Co., Chicago.
Rare two-horn phonograph, oak
case, ca. 1907. 18" x 9" x 13".
....$2,200

Edison Ambrola phonograph, in handcrafted mahogany cabinet, complete with cylinders in drawers, ca. 1908-1912. 50" x 22" x 22".
......................................$2,300

Edison Ambrola Model 50. Cylinder machine made for vertical-cut four-minute records, ca. 1913. Mahogany case. 15" x 20" x 16".
....$500

Victor table model, with inside or folded horn, ca. 1909. Oak case 16" x 16" x 9".
....$195

Swanson portable phonograph. Hollow tone arm, folds and fits in front compartment, ca. 1909. Black leatherette case. 11" x 11" x 10".
....$250

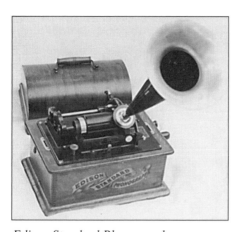

Edison Standard Phonograph.
Base, 12¼" x 8¼" x 5".
....$625

Cylinder music box, walnut case.
Plays six tunes. Length 13¼".
....$600

Symphonion disc music box,
walnut case. Width 16". Ht.
9½". Disc size 10½".
..................................$1,300

Edison cylinder Model B
phonograph. Last patent
date 1907. Ht. 37".
....................................$300

Musical

Thomas Edison tabletop phonograph in working order, with oak case and approx. 45 cylinders. 12" x 15" x 15" high.
....**$575**

Bing Pigmyphone, a miniature tin replica of a full-size phonograph, manufactured ca. 1918.
....**$495**

Mahogany tabletop gramophone manufactured by the Victrola Talking Machine Co., Camden, N.J. Labelled "His Master's Voice." Crank driven, two front drawers, 15½" x 19" x 15" high.
....**$350**

LEFT:
*Phonograph. Maker
unknown. Ht. lid up
25". Width 14¾".*
..........................**$195**

*Record cabinet, birch and
mahogany. Ht. 43½".
Width 19".*
....................................**$250**

*Victor phonograph, quarter oak,
mid to late 1920s. Ht. 8½".*
....**$225**

*Edison phonograph. Oak case.
ca.1909. Ht. lid up 24", W. 12¾".*
....**$425**

*Edison Fireside phonograph Model
B, patented 1896 and 1905. Length
10½". Length of horn 21".*
....**$625**

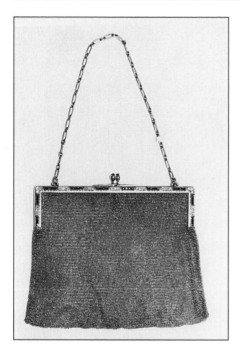

American 14K gold purse with diamonds and sapphires, ca. 1915.
....$6,500

Late-Victorian handmade beaded bag of possible Austrian origin, highlighted by sapphires, rubies and emeralds, and resting on a silver gilt frame. It was made as a gift from Anna Held - actress and wife of American theatrical producer Florenz Ziegfeld, creator of Ziegfeld Follies - to her sister Maria Held. On the front the name Maria Held is done in beads while the initials A.H. appear on the back.
....$2,500

English purse with beaded clasp and floral decoration, ca. 1880.
....$95

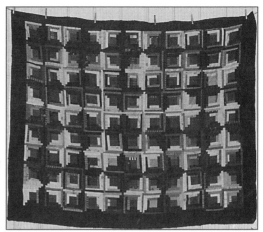

Oxford County quilt, which was made as a "Wedding Quilt" by Mabel Brooks of Eastwood, Ontario around 1910. She made a quilt for each of her sons, but this one wasn't used as the boy never married.
....**$425**

Waterloo County quilt from Elmira, Ontario, dating to the early 19th century, with strong graphic design.
...................................**$695**

Mennonite "trip around the world" quilt, ca. 1900, from Waterloo County, Ontario.
.....................................**$975**

Oval hooked rug from Middlesex County, ca. 1895, with central leaf and flower decoration.
.....................................**$375**

Waterloo County Mennonite rug, 1908.
............................**$495**

Top: Quebec-origin hooked rug with rooster, dated 1938.
................................**$435**
Bottom: Hooked rug from Port Hope with hen & rooster, last quarter 19th century.
.....................................**$595**

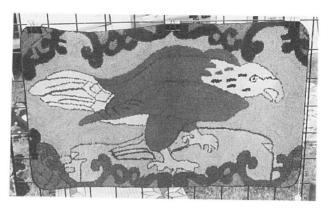

Yarn hooked rug, "Perched Eagle," ca. 1910.
....**$275**

Hooked rug showing horse within a horseshoe, surrounded by green leaves on a grey background, ca. 1920.
....**$525**

Hooked rug from Ontario, possibly Vittoria area, ca. 1900.
.............................**$250**

*Hooked rug,
"Clydesdale Horses."
...........................$475*

*Rare chicken hooked rug,
originating in Quebec,
ca. 1820.
...............................$575*

*Very rare Quebec
hooked rug with
a skunk as the
central figure,
ca. 1930.
...................$750*

Attractive small hooked rug (14 x 10 inches), probably from Quebec or the Maritimes, ca. 1890.
....................................$250

Hooked rug, "Swans with Lily Pads" from Simcoe County, ca. 1940.
..................................$175

Hooked rug from Quebec with a very folksy farm scene.
......................$795

Hooked rug, "Sailing Ship with Seagulls," from Oshawa area, ca. 1900.
.........................**$535**

Hooked rug with unusual subject matter, "A Family of Skunks," originating in the Kingston area, ca. 1935.
...............................**$825**

Hooked rug, "The Country Cottage," from Nova Scotia, late 1930s.
.................**$225**

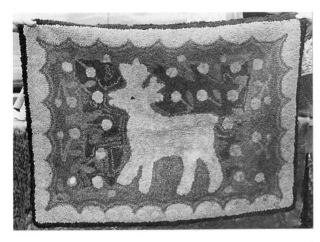

Hooked rug, originating from Ontario, ca. 1920.
..............................$1,650

Hooked rug, originating from Simcoe County.
................................$125

Very attractive Grenfell rug from Nova Scotia, ca. 1900.
............................$950

Graphically designed hooked rug from Brant County, ca. 1870.
....**$650**

Grenfell hooked rug in silk, depicting a Windjammer in full sail.
....**$1,700**

A strikingly colourful hooked rug from Quebec, showing country houses
(18" x 68"), ca. 1940.
....**$1,250**

Grenfell hooked "Bear" rug (17" x 24").
..................................$1,650

Contour-edged circular hooked rug of floral design, originating in the London area, ca. 1930.
....$260

Grenfell hooked rug from Labrador, produced in a factory employing local residents, ca. 1925.
....$1,780

Hooked rug from Summerside, P.E.I.
...................**$875**

Hooked rug, showing a beaver on a branch, Quebec, ca. 1920.
....**$350**

"Three Bears" hooked rug.
..............**$375**

Floral and geometric hooked rug, ca. 1930. Originated from Massachusetts.
........................$2,600

Hooked rug, Ontario origin, 1940.
....$295

Beaded pincushion, 6" square, dated 1906.
....$65

Sewer's companion mahogany with diamond pattern inlay, ca. 1900. Four spool holders, pincushion and drawer. Ht. 3½" x 7" long.
....$125

Sewer's companion walnut carousel, ca. 1900, holds twelve spools with pincushion on top. Ht. 8".
....$135

Counter scale, brass scoop, beam and sliding poise, cast iron base.
....$175

Postal scale, brass pans and weights on wood base. Length 10½".
.....................................$225

Scales

Postal scale, black enamel with gilt trim. Round slanted dial.
....$75

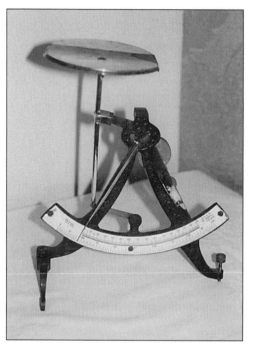

Postal scales. German, made for the Danish market, ca. 1870, with adjustable weight - up for the lighter top scale, and placed down for the heavier bottom scale.
....**$175-$200**

Postal scales of Italian origin, ca. 1870. Brass on wooden base.
.....................................**$400-$475**

Hand held scale. Brass pans stamped "Dr. Jekill," steel beam, brass weights, excise stamp "GR" (George Rex), ca. 1920. Complete with 10 weights and wooden box.
....$195

Apothecary scale, by H. Troemner, Philadelphia, PA. Brass pans, marble bed, balance gauge in front. Dated 1884. Length 17".
....$240

Scales

Balance scale from Holland, ca. 1870. 5 kilo capacity, brass pans on cast iron base.
....**$185**

Confectioner's scale. British, by Hunt & Co., late 1800s. Brass weight pan, other pan and bed are marble. Wood base. Length 22".
....**$265**

Dayton Counter Scale by the Dayton Computing Co., Dayton, Ohio, 0-2 pounds capacity, 10 cents to $1.00 per pound. Gold colour cast iron with brass scoop. Last patent date, March 27, 1906.
.....................................**$225**

*Brass scales. English, late
19th century. Ht. 23".*
....$275

*Even balance brass scales,
early 1900s. Ht. 18".*
....................................$225

Scales

*Pair of scales in cast iron with copper scoop pan and brass
pan for weights. Ht. with pan 19".*
....$285

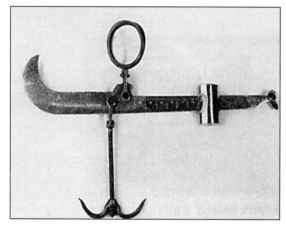

Hanging scale, 0-25 pounds, brass beam & sliding poise (balance), steel hook. British, late 1800s, stamped "Osborne & Co., Hamilton" & "VR." Length 19".
....**$125**

Miller's scale, used to measure moisture content of grain. Brass, ¹/₁₆ bushell pail with beam. British, by W & J.G. Greenley. Government stamped. Length of beam 12".
.............................**$250-$300**

Left: Hanging scale, 0-12 pounds, mid-1800s. Tin cylinder, steel hook. Length 12".
...................................**$35**
Right: Spring scale, late 1800s, early 1900s. Cast iron, embossed wheat, oats, barley, peas and flax. Length 12".
...................................**$48**

The Renfrew Machinery Co. made the wheelbarrow type scale from 1911-1932. Other Companies making similar scales in this period, The Pembroke Scale Co. and The Chatham Scale Co., made a comparatively small number.

The portable scales illustrated on these pages were once an essential item on the farm, weighing grain, milk, small livestock, etc. Although they went out of general use on the farm about 30 years ago, they now have a new lease of life as decorative and useful items in the home, being much in demand for tables, stands for flowers and for the display of antiques and curios. Often they have lain idle for many years, but being made of good quality materials, well refinished ones command good prices.

Renfrew maple weight type grain scale in original condition.
....$795
Slide scale type was patented in 1929.

Wool winder with measuring mechanism.
....$390

Wool winder. Ht. 46".
...........................$240

Pine wool winder. Ht. 31".
...............................$215

Pine wool winder, ca. 1880.
....$225

Wool winder, ca. 1860.
Excellent condition.
.............................**$290**

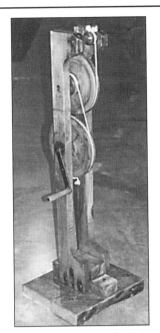

Small Quebec wool winder,
late 1800s. Ht. 24".
.................................**$195**

Triple gear wool winder. Unusual
type from Eastern Canada. Ash
and pine, early 1900s. Ht. 38".
..............................**$320**

Quebec wool winder with counter. Oak
and pine, ca. 1880. Ht. 46".
.....................................**$250**

Spinning

Small spinning wheel in original paint (incomplete), signed "A. Choquet." Ht. 40".
....$435

Spinning wheel, mid-19th century (as found), signed "A. Choquet." Ht. 38".
....$435

Small spinning wheel from Eganville, Ontario. Ht. 35". Length 32".
....$425

Spinning wheel from the Ottawa Valley, ca. 1860.
....$575

Quebec origin wool winder, ca. 1875.
....**$185**

Spinning wheel. Ht. 50" with 19" diam. wheel. Good working order.
....**$310**

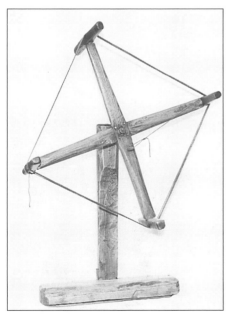

Spinning wheel, all original. Length 48".
....**$395**

Unusual squirrel-cage wool winder from Peel County, Ontario, ca. 1850.
.....................................**$225**

LEFT:
Spinning wheel (refinished),
ca. 1840. Ht. 30".
.....................................$465

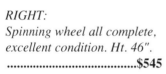

RIGHT:
Spinning wheel all complete,
excellent condition. Ht. 46".
....$545

LEFT:
Small spinning wheel
(incomplete). Length 34".
...............................$395

RIGHT:
Spinning wheel.
Ht. 37", Length 37".
..........................$485

Brantford Stoneware Manufacturing Co. five-gallon crock dating from the period 1894-1906.
....$250

W.E. Welding three-gallon stoneware crock from Brantford, Ontario, dating from the period 1873-1894.
....$375

Left: Blue flower decorated crock, W.E. Welding of Brantford, Ontario.
....$385
Right: Blue flower decorated crock, E.L. Farrar of Iberville, Quebec.
....$345

Stoneware/Pottery

The arrival of the Farrars around 1830, newly emigrated potters from the U.S.A., marked an important step in the history of pottery in Canada.

The Farrars were well established with their pottery works at St. John in Lower Canada by 1840, and had been followed by several other emigrants specializing in ceramics, including the Bells of Scotland and the Howisons. The region became known as "The Staffordshire of Canada," with the Farrars maintaining their pottery works there until around 1925. They marked their articles with "E.L. Farrar" or simply "St. John" or "Iberville, P.Q."

Four gallon crock, "E.L. Farrar, Iberville, P.Q." Blue floral decoration on tan.
....$235

Six gallon crock, "W.E. Welding, Brantford, Ont." Blue floral decoration on tan.
....$275

Five gallon crock, "Warner & Co., Toronto." Blue floral decoration on tan.
....$265

Two gallon crock, with lid, "H. Schuler, Paris, Ont." Blue flowers on tan.
....$395

LEFT:
Two gallon crock, ca. 1880,
originating from the London,
Ontario, area.
....$345

RIGHT:
Prince Edward island crock
with unusual snake
decoration, 1880-1890.
.....................................$330

Canadian stoneware one gallon jug, Wesley Bullen,
Grocers & Wine Merchant, Belleville & Trenton.
....$285

Five gallon crock, "Medalta Potteries Ltd., Medicine Hat, Alberta."
......................................$75

Small crock, "Medalta Potteries Ltd., Medicine Hat, Alberta." Ht. 4".
....$65

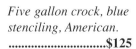

Five gallon crock, blue stenciling, American.
.............................$125

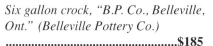

Four gallon crock, "G.B. & Co., London" (Glass Bros. & Co.)
....$195

Six gallon crock, "B.P. Co., Belleville, Ont." (Belleville Pottery Co.)
....$185

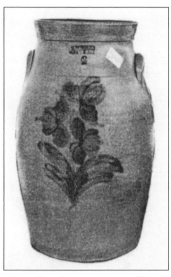

Six gallon butter churn, "H. Schuler, Paris, Ont." Blue floral decoration.
...................................$380

Five gallon butter churn, "W.E. Welding, Brantford, Ont." Blue floral decoration.
...................................$330

Eight gallon butter churn, "B.P. Co., Belleville, Ont." (Belleville Pottery Co.)
...................................$200

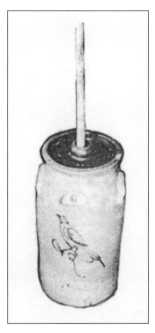

Six gallon butter churn, "Hart Bros. & Lazier, Belleville, Ont." Bird on branch in blue.
...........................$685

Two gallon stoneware jug with unusual floral decoration, Welding & Belding, Brantford, Ont., 1867-1872.
....**$1,150**

Decorated stoneware jug, Morton & Co., Brantford, Ontario, 1849-1856.
..................................**$730**

Rare merchant jug from the Toronto Market Square, ca. 1870. Impressed with William Strachan, Wine and Spirit Merchant.
....**$475**

Four gallon jug, "St. John (Pottery), Quebec." Blue decoration on beige ground.
....**$570**

Three gallon jug, "Albert Gauthier, Montreal." Tan with blue floral decoration.
....**$195**

One gallon jug, "Thomas Furlong, Wine Merchant, St. John, N.B." Tan.
..............................**$180**

One gallon jug, "Georges Couture Hotel, Ste. Julie Sta." Tan.
....**$170**

LEFT:
Kingston merchant stoneware jug dated 1861. Manufactured by S. Skinner & Co., marked Abraham Foster, Wine & Spirit Merchant, Kingston, Canada West.
....$650

ABOVE:
Two gallon stoneware jug made in the United States by Ottman Bos & Co. in Fort Edward, N.Y., for J.A. Russell on Queen St. in Fredericton, ca. 1871.
....$800

LEFT:
Three gallon stoneware jug marked G.I. Lazier, Picton, C.W. with the date 1870 enclosed in an incised heart.
....$1,100

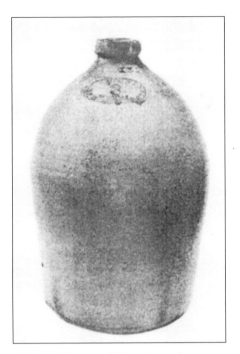

Three gallon jug, "Hart Bros. &
Lazier, Belleville, Ont." Tan.
....$250

Two gallon jug, "J. Casey & CO.,
General Merchant, Eganville." Brown.
....$120

Molasses jugs, brown.
Left: Ht. 8½".
...............................$45
Right: Ht. 9½".
...............................$48

Ovoid stoneware jug with cobalt blue floral motif, marked H. Schuler, Paris, Ont.
....$790

Rare two gallon stoneware jug with bird decoration marked Eberhardt & Halm, Toronto, C.W., dating to the period 1863-1865.
......................................$6,750

Canadian stoneware jug with impressed marks, L. Thorne, Wine & Spirit Merchand [sic] Seaforth, Ont.
....$255

Red wing crock.
...........................$85
These turn up quite often in the Prairies. This one was in Nanton, Alberta.

Two gallon jug, "Medalta,
Medicine Hat." Brown/tan.
.....................................$95

Three gallon jug, "E.T. Sandall,
Wine & Spirit Merchant, 523-525
Yonge St." Brown/tan.
....$150

One gallon jug, "H.F. Morrison,
Wholesale Liquor Merchant,
Dauphin, Man." Brown/white.
....$175

One gallon jug, "J.A. Smith,
Wine Merchant, Estavan."
Brown/white.
.................................$125

Stoneware/Pottery

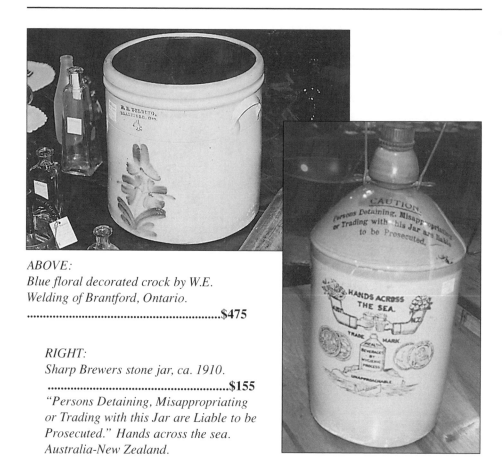

ABOVE:
Blue floral decorated crock by W.E.
Welding of Brantford, Ontario.
....$475

RIGHT:
Sharp Brewers stone jar, ca. 1910.
....$155
"Persons Detaining, Misappropriating
or Trading with this Jar are Liable to be
Prosecuted." Hands across the sea.
Australia-New Zealand.

Mixing bowl, Medalta Pottery.
....$175

Insect trap plate, dated March 14th,
1867.
....$425

LEFT:
Old Homestead ginger beer bottle, manufactured by the International Drug Co., St. Stephen, N.B., and Calais, Maine.
.......................................$45-$80

BELOW:
Atkinson
(a) $800-$1000; (b) $300-$400; (c) $300-$400
William Atkinson was a beverage bottler of long standing in Guelph, operating from 1861 to 1899, taking over the business of Thomas Atkinson - first at part lot 110 Macdonell Street and later at 52 Liverpool Street. Impressed in the early hand-formed blob top bottle is "W. Atkinson, Guelph C.W." The blue stamping on the cream coloured bottle in the centre reads "W. Atkinson, Ginger Beer, Guelph, Ontario." The marking on the latest of the Atkinson bottles at the right says "W. Atkinson, Ginger Beer, Guelph." Impressed into the clay at the bottom of this later bottle is the name of the Scottish bottle manufacturer - H. Kennedy, Barrowfield Potteries, Glasgow.

Royal Haegar pottery lamp with matching shade, 1950-60. Both decorated with angel fish.
....**$395**

Doulton Burslem commemorative pitcher in blue and brown. Queen Victoria's Diamond Jubilee, 1897.
....**$625**

Copeland - late Spode, 1897 Diamond Jubilee teapot in dark green with relief medallion of Queen Victoria.
....**$795**
Not shown: Matching pitcher, 5¼" high.
....**$350**

German grey stoneware Bellarmine tankard, with bearded mask, 16¼" high, with the main frieze depicting various family coat-of-arms, ca. 1880.
....$495

German grey stoneware jug 12½" high with blue, green and brown glaze decoration depicting a bearded figure holding aloft a foaming tankard of ale.
....$395

Pair of German grey stoneware jugs 10¼" high, each highlighted with an inscription within a large cartouche. Cobalt blue floral decoration.
......................$250 ea.

LEFT:
Triple box telephone, centre speaking box patented by Black in U.S. and licensed for use in Canada. The two red bands on the receiver indicate that the phone was for use in Canada. Pine and walnut box, ca. 1881.
....$1,750

RIGHT:
Long distance bridging phone made for Bell Canada by Northern Electric, Montreal, 1890s. For use from town to town and usually located in telephone office or store, not homes. Pine back, remainder walnut, glass mouthpiece. Ht. 32".
....$850

Canadian Independent Telephone Co., made from 1902-1910. Oak cased phone with picture frame front and cathedral back, bakelite receiver and mouthpiece. Has external connectors and lightning arrester. Ht. 25".
....$450

First single box phone by Northern Electric. Oak picture frame case, bakelite receiver. Made 1900-1912. Ht. 23".
....$350

Space saver wall model with 45 degree shelf by Northern Electric, Montreal. Made in oak case, 1919-35 and in maple case to start of World War II. Ht. 20".
....**$275**

Single box plain front phone by Northern Electric. Long goose-neck arm, bakelite receiver & mouthpiece. Ht. 20".
....**$300**

LEFT:
Daffodil type phone. Nickel plated phone by Northern Electric Mfg. Co., Montreal, 1898-1912. Bakelite receiver. Ht. 12".
.................................**$250**

CENTRE:
Daffodil type phone made for Connecticut Telephone Co. by Western Electric, Chicago, 1914-1925. Nickel plated head, black painted base, bakelite receiver.
.....................................**$200**

RIGHT:
Daffodil type dial phone by Northern Electric, Montreal and Toronto, 1924-30.
..........................**$350**

Telephones

Model 302 square base phone by Northern Electric, 1937-42. Heavy black painted spelter base.
...........................$95

Model 202 oval base phone by Northern Electric, Montreal and Toronto, 1928-32.
....$125

Note: The Northern Electric & Mfg. Co. Ltd., Montreal, started manufacturing telephones in 1880. In 1912 a factory was opened in Toronto under the same name. In 1914 the name was changed to Northern Electric Company Limited and in 1978 became Northern Telecom Limited.

Three slot pay phone by Northern Electric. Black painted metal case with chrome fittings, plastic receiver. First model with theft proof coin shute. Made with minor changes from 1953-73.
....$200

LEFT:
Wall dial phone by Northern Electric, 1924-30. The wall phone of the same period as the daffodil desk phone. Painted wood case. Ht. 9".
....$225

RIGHT:
Commercial desk phone by Northern Electric, 1932-50. Mounted on wood display stand, but came with metal bracket for fitting on desk.
....$150

Danish telephone converted for use in Canada, by Bell Telephone Co.
....**$325**

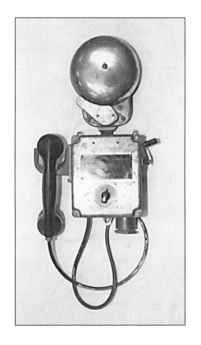

Ship's intercom/phone by Henschel Corp., Amesbury, Mass., U.S.A., 1915-20.
...................................**$240**

Dictograph-office intercom, 1930s. Walnut case, 8½" x 8½" x 6½".
....**$195**

Tea tin, Ocean Blend Tea Co.,
Toronto, 1930s. 4" x 4" x 6½".
....$45

Lipton's tea tin, black with gold and
silver illustrations. Ht. 6".
....$18

Coffee or tea canister. Red,
decorated with Chinese motif. Ht. 6".
....$15

Tea container. English,
1940s, maroon, gold, red and
blue. Ht. 6½".
....$35

Potato chip tin, late 1930s. American, yellow with black and red. Ht. 11½".
....$35

Riley's toffee canister. English, 1920s, orange, purple and gold. Ht. 15".
....$95

Top/left: Smiles & Chuckles buttermilk wafers tin, ca. 1918-20. Orange. Diam. 11".
....$65

Top/right: Blue Bird marshmallow tin, 1920s. Yellow and blue. Diam. 10".
....$70

Left: John Bull candy tin, 1930s. "Greetings from Canada" label and names of Canadian cities. Diam. 3".
....$35

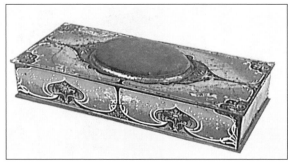

Rowntree's cocoa tin, blue and gold with red velvet pincushion in lid. 1¾" x 4" x 10".
....$55

Reno coffee tin, one pound. Blue and white.
...................................$30

Castle Blend tea tin. Head office, Montreal, ca. 1920. Decorated with four different castles. 7" x 7" x 7".
....$40

Toddy tin, A. Wander Co., Peterborough, Ontario, early 1940s. Red with cream labels. Ht. 4".
....$25

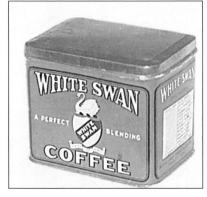

White Swan coffee tin, White Swan Spices & Cereals Ltd., Toronto, 1920s. Red and white.
....$35

Keene's mustard tin. English, early 1900s. Litho-tin illustrating the life and awards of Admiral Nelson. 5½" x 8" x 6".
....$145

Huntley & Palmer biscuit tin. English, ca. 1901. Chinese style illustrating storks and bamboo. 9" x 5½" x 3½".
....$130

Cosmetic tin, 1930s, with portrait of Gloria Swanson. Diam. 5".
....$45

ABOVE:
Coronation souvenir, 1953. Blue, portrait of Queen Elizabeth, gold trim. Ht. 5".
....$18

LEFT:
Oxo tin. Elizabeth II Coronation, June 2, 1958. Red. 1" x 3½" x 2½".
....$18

Toleware store canister, by the Dominion Stamping Works, Montreal. Stencilled lettering, "Select Pepper," and hand painted horse head on mustard colour ground. Late 1800s. Lid missing. Ht. 9". Diam. 6".
....**$95**

Tin shaker, lettered "Flour" on a red ground, late 1800s. Ht. 4".
....**$35**

Baking powder tins, early 1900s.
....**$25-$50.**
Left to Right:
"Superior," *York Trading Co Ltd., Toronto. Red lettering on mustard colour label.*
"Poudre a Pate," *J.W. Page, Quebec, QC. Unopened with contents.*
"Morning Glory," *full colour flowers.*

Exmoor Hunt Mixture, W.O. Biggs & Co. 4¼" x 3¼".
....$20

Davenports Medium Navy Cut. 5" x 3".
....$25

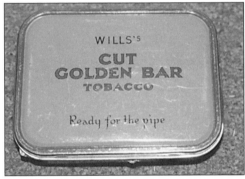

Will's Cut Golden Bar Tobacco, mf'd by W.D. & H.O. Wills Branch of the Imperial Tobacco Co., (of Great Britain and Ireland) Ltd. 4¼" x 3¼".
....$20

Tom Long Tobacco, W. & F. Faulkner, London, S.E. 1. 4¼" x 3¼".
....$22

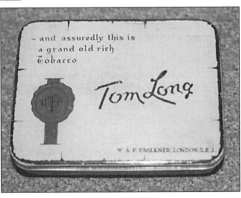

Tins

Black Cat Cigarettes, mf'd by Carreras Ltd., Arcadia Works, City Road, E.C., London, England. 4½" x 3".
....$20

Forest and Stream Tobacco, Imperial Tobacco Co. Litho-tin with two fishermen with dog in canoe. Rare. Ht. 4".
....$265
Note: Other illustrations worth less.

Brompton Hospital Lozenges, Smith Kendon Ltd., London, S.W. 1. 3⅛" x 2¼".
......................................$12

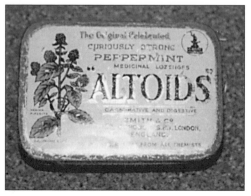

Altoids Peppermint Medicinal Lozenges, Smith & Co., London, England. 3⅛" x 2¼".
....$8

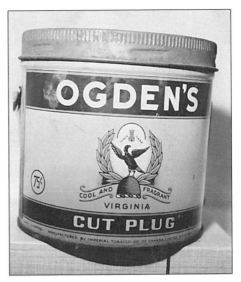

Chateau Gay, a cool, mellow pipe tobacco.
....$15
(Also marketed as Chateau Quebec)

Ogden's Cut Plug, manufactured by Imperial Tobacco Company of Canada.
....$55

Canada Straight cigarette tobacco, manufactured by Royal Canadian Tobacco Co., Toronto.
....$60

Daily Mail, a mild cigarette tobacco, made in Canada for Consolidated Tobacco Inc., Montreal.
....$40

Tins

*Mackintosh's Quality Street.
Ht. 3". Diam. 5".*
.....................................$18

*Huntley & Palmers Biscuits,
"Noddy, Sally Skittle & Wobbly
Man." Ht. 1¼". Diam. 5".*
....$25

*Huntley & Palmers Biscuits,
"Noddy & Big Ears." Ht. 1¼".
Diam. 5".*
....$25

Oxo Cubes. 3" x 2".
.........................$12

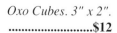

Christie's Biscuits, Christie, Brown and Company Limited, by appointment to their Excellencies The Governor-General and Viscountess Willingdon.
....**$145**

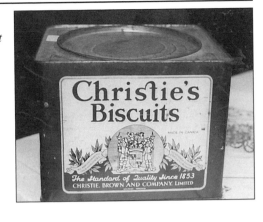

Riley's toffee canister, orange, purple and gold. English, 1920s. Ht. 15".
.....................................**$95**

Keene's Mustard litho-tin with scenes of Canada, Australia, India, South Africa and England, plus illustrations of the Order of the Indian Empire, 1890-1900. 5½" x 8" x 6".
....**$135**

T. Eaton Co. Limited breadbox, marked with both Toronto and Winnipeg, ca. 1910.
.............................**$295**

Tins

Candy tin, Harry Horne Co., Toronto, Circus Club Mallows. Ht. 7½".
....$55

Christie Brown & Co. Limited, Toronto, Montreal, biscuit tin dated Oct. 1915. "From the Land of the Maple, The Canadian Expeditionary force."
..........................$68

Bristol souvenir of the Coronation of Their Majesties King George V and Queen Mary. J.S. Fry & Sons, chocolate & cocoa.
Inside: Presented by the Lord Mayor & Citizens of Bristol 22nd June, 1911. 6" x 3½".
..........................$65

Christie, Brown Co. biscuit tin, August 1917, sent to troops in France. Titled "The Canadian Expeditionary Force" and listed all major battles up to that date.
....$75

Promotional candy container tins issued by William Neilson Ltd., Toronto, around 1990, containing 240 grams of Jersey Milk, Crispy Crunch or Caramilk, and sold as a premium through Canadian Tire service outlets. Ht. 5½".
....$12 ea.

Tins

Quaker White Oats, a stunning tin in great condition.
...........................$55
Watkins Pepper tin.
...........................$35
(J & B Scotch Whisky jug by Wade.)
...........................$49

Sugar/cinnamon shaker. White tin decorated with apples, red cap. "Decoware" by Continental Can Co. Ht. 3¾".
....**$15**

Felix the Cat pail. Ht. 7".
...................................**$18**

Large selection of tins, including:

Red Indian Oil, Frontenac Oil Co.
.........................**$85**

Meerschaum Cut Plug, blue & red (full).
..........................**$42**

Imperial Oil (full).
.........................**$42**

Other prices range from $15-$85.

Child's tea set, complete for four. German origin, ca. 1900.
....**$285**

Victorian Staffordshire child's 14-piece tea set, "Girl with pet goat" in pink and white transfer ware, ca. 1870.
....**$950**

Toys

Doll Buggies

Wicker doll buggy, ca. 1920.
....$225

Unusual handmade doll
buggy, ca. 1930.
...............................$175

Wicker doll buggy, early 1900s.
....$235

Wicker doll's carriage. Ht. to top of hood 34". Length 35".
....$285

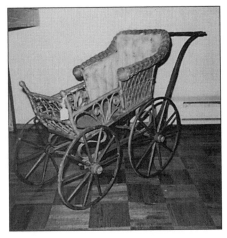

Victorian wicker doll carriage with roll around back and original quilted silk lining.
....$545

Unusual wicker sulkie-type doll buggy, all original, ca. 1905.
...........................$325

Handmade oak child's doll cart from Ontario County, ca. 1890.
...........................$295

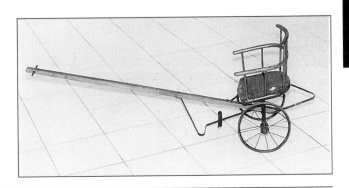

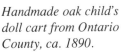
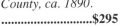

Toys

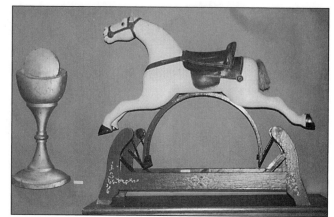

Victorian rocking horse.
..........................**$1,800**

Combination
rocking and pull
horse, late 1800s.
.....................**$895.**

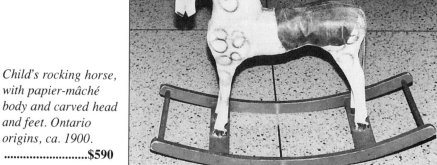

Child's rocking horse,
with papier-mâché
body and carved head
and feet. Ontario
origins, ca. 1900.
..........................**$590**

Toy fire engine, 1960 era.
...................................**$65**

Toy shell tanker by Majorette, France. Driver cabin hinges.
.........................**$48**

Toy open trailer by Siku, Germany. Driver cabin hinges.
..............................**$48**

A colourful Schieble open touring car, ca. 1914.
..................**$1,295**

Toys

Rodeo Joe tin windup toy from the 1960s.
.........................$350

Toy ferris wheel by Chein in almost mint condition.
.....................................$750

French Unis doll seated in a wagon which is pulled by a mechanical horse, ca. 1880.
....$495

Battery operated Cragstan melody band drummer, 1950s.
....**$195**

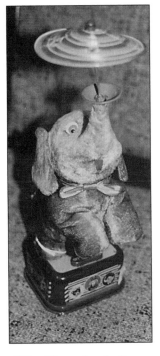

"The Circus Jumbo," mechanical elephant with spinning umbrella, late 1940s.
...........................**$295**

Bobby, the drinking bear, sitting on a tree stump with a bottle of "Coo-Coo." Battery operated. Great find for the bear collector! In need of mechanical repair.
....**$165**
(In good condition price would be $650)

Toys

Checker board and Nine Men's Morris, three colours on pine board, with storage boxes (swivel lids). Home crafted piece (not original checkers) from Kingston, Nova Scotia, ca. 1900.
....**$2,275**

Toy general store, made by Wolverine, ca. 1930.
....**$385**

Child's handcrafted doll house made in 1927 by the grandfather of the owner. Original twig log construction, oak floor and door with brass knob, chimney hand carved and coloured to represent bricks, roof tiles made from tar paper, wired for electricity. Very folksy.
.....................................**$395**

Unusual child's pedal toy in the shape of a biplane. Obviously made for "Pat." $2,200

Clown money bank, composite material, 1930s. Ht. 12".
....$35

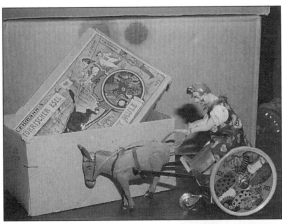

The Balky Mule by the German toy company Lehmann, 1903. This colorful wind-up toy is in excellent condition complete with original box.
....$550

Iron engine with brass bell and fittings. Keystone Rail Rd., Milton, Boston.
...................................$395

Toys

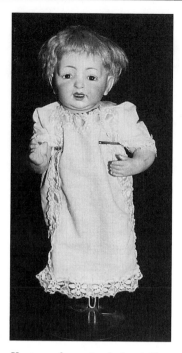

"Bobbi-Mae Swing & Sway Doll" inspired by Sammy Kaye and made by Wondercraft Co., New York City in the 1940s.

Kestner character baby doll #211 with original blonde hair.
....$775

....$175

Gebruder Heubach character baby, ca. 1910, measuring 9".
....$375

English walnut miniature canopy bed, ca. 1860, and blonde Martha Washington doll with an American china head and cloth body, ca. 1875.
...................................$425

German-origin bisque head, composition body doll, ca. 1900, by Bruno Schmidt.
....$795

Gerbruder Heubach doll titled "The Pouting Heubach," ca. 1910.
...............................$650

German, marked R.A., doll standing 16" tall.
....$565

Toys

Chad Valley "Princess Elizabeth"
doll, 1930s. Very rare.
............................$1,450-$1,650

1920s German S&H porcelain
doll. The clothing pre-dates the
doll by 30 years. The lace gown
is in lovely condition, of floral net
lace trimmed with blue silk
ribbons.
....$700

Norah Wellings sailor doll,
English, 1920. Ht. 30".
...............................$375

Norah Wellings sailor doll with
inscription "R.M.S. Invernia" on its hat.
....$395

Nisbet "Golly." Ht. 19".
.................................$110

Sherlock Holmes doll, ca. 1960.
....$135

American stuffed clown doll,
ca. 1920.
..................................$225

Mint condition Mickey Mouse Club
cloth stuffed toy by Knickerbocker
with original tag.
....$95

Toys

*One ton Army tank 641 (G)
1954-62. Olive green.
Length 3".*
....**$65**

*7.2 inch Howitzer 693 (G)
1958-67.*
....**$45**

*Covered transport wagon
151 b (G) 1946-48.*
....**$125**
*Anti-aircraft gun mounted on
trailer. 161 b (G) 1946-48.*
....**$135**

*Left: Hotchkiss Willys
Jeep 80 b (F) 1958-59.
Length 3".*
..............................**$75**
*Right: Austin military
truck, 30 sm (G), 1952-
53. Length 4".*
..............................**$175**

ABOVE:
Thorneycroft Mighty Antar tank transporter 660 (H) 1956. Length 6¾", with trailer length 12".
....$275
Centurion tank 651 (G) 1954. Length 5¼".
....$115

Spectrum Pursuit vehicle 104 (J) 1968-77. Fantasy vehicle from the Thunderbirds TV series. Length 6½".
....$75

Front: Supermarine swift fighter 734 (G) 1955-62. Length 2½".
..............................$60 ea.
Back: Glouster Javelin fighter 735 (G) 1956-66. Length 4".
..............................$65 ea.

Left: Shooting Star jet fighter 733 (G) 1954-62. Length 2¼".
..............................$35
Right: Vickers Viscount airliner 708 (G) 1957-65. Wingspan 6½".
..............................$45

Toys

Muir Hill 2 WL loader 437 (G).
....$35

Climax Conveyancer fork lift 404 (G)
1967-79. (Roll cage and driver missing)
....$20

Elevator loader 964 (G) 1952-54.
Ht. 6½".
....$175

Coventry Climax fork lift truck 14 c (G)
1949-53. Orange, green & black. Length 4".
....$110

Field Marshall tractor 301 (G)
1954-65. Length 3".
....$45

Hay rack 27 k (G) 1958.
......................................$45

Mamod steam tractor, made in
England, 1960s. Mint in box.
Length 10".
......................................$240

Mamod steam wagon made in
England, 1960s. Mint in box.
Length 11".
......................................$230

Toys

Three ton army wagon
621 (G) 1954-63. Olive
green. Length 4½".
..............................$70

Weeko tipping farm trailer
319 (G) 1961-70.
..................................$35

Left: Foden 8-wheel flat
truck 902 (G) 1955-60.
Length 7½".
..............................$165
Right: Foden 8-wheel
flat truck with chains
905 (G) 1955-66
(3 stakes & chain
missing). Length 7½".
..............................$125

Bedford TK coal truck 425 (G)
1964-69 (accessories - black
coal sacks missing).
....$50

Left: Triumph 2000, 135 (G)
1963-69. Length 4".
.....................................**$20-$35**
Right: Articulated truck 424 (G)
1963-66. Length 7".
.....................................**$30-$50**

Ford Model T (1908) 475 (G)
1964-68. Length 3½".
..................................**$28-55**

Aston Martin DB5, 110 (H)
1966-70. Length 4½".
..............................**$16-28**

Land Rover 340 (G) 1954-71. Length 3½".
....**$16-$28**
Land Rover trailer 341 (G) 1954-71. Length 3".
....**$12-$18**

Toys

Model Cars

Plymouth Estate Car 344 (G)
1954-61 (chipped paint).
Length 4".
....$85

Left: Standard Vanguard 40 e
(G) 1948-53. Length 4".
....$75
Right: Rover 7S, 140 b (G)
1951-53. Length 4".
....$70

Dinky Toys delivery
service car
transporter 982 (G)
1954-1963.
....................$250

Left to Right:
Nash Rambler Fire Chief 257 (H) 1961-68. Length 4".
....$27-$45
Morris 1100, 140 (G) 1963-69. Length 3½".
....$15-$22
Volkswagen 1300 Sedan Deluxe 129 (H) 1965-76. Length 3".
....$18-$35
Triumph TR7, 211 (G) 1975-79. Length 3¾".
....$10-$15

Left: Daimler Ambulance 253 (G) 1954-64. Length 4".
....**$20-$36**
Right: M.G. Midget 108 (G) 1955-59. Length 3¼".
....**$13-$28**

Commer Fire Engine 955 (G) 1955-69.
Length 5½". Red truck with silver ladder.
....**$200**

Left: Jaguar "D" Type 238 (G) 1957-65. Length 3¼".
....**$18-$30**
Right: Vauxhall Cresta 164 (G) 1957-60. Length 3¾".
....**$22-$35**

Toys

A.A. motorcycle patrol (Automobile Association, England) 44 b (G) 1935-53. Length 2".
....**$65 ea.**

Dinky breakdown lorry (Commer chassis), 1945-53, with its original box. Length 5".
....**$295**
See the original price of $1.29 handwritten on top of the box.

Bedford CA Ovaltine van 481 (G) 1955-59. Length 3½".
....**$125**

Trojan Oxo van 31 d (G) 1953 (tires missing). Length 3½".
....**$100**

Pine sleigh with iron runners and rails. Converts to four seats. Late 1800s. Refinished.
....$625

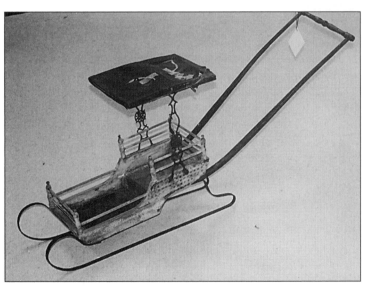

Primitive child's sleigh, most likely home made.
....$590

Transportation

Snowshoes, sinew meshing and leather bindings. Stamped "Wallinford VT." 10" x 36".
....$85

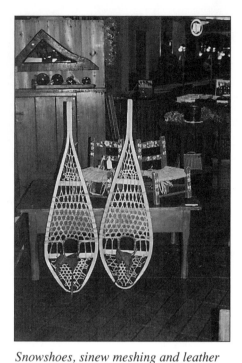

Snowshoes, sinew meshing and leather bindings, Canadian made.
....$95

Victorian wicker pet carrier with wrought-iron gate.
......................................$265

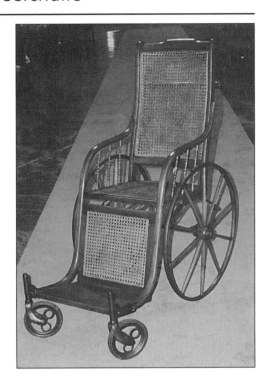

*Oak wheelchair 4' tall in
perfect condition, ca. 1875.*
..................................**$750**

*World War I, military
hospital wheelchair, wood
with wire spoke wheels.*
...................................**$275**

Transportation

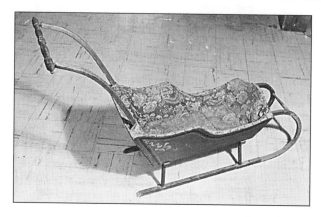

Child's sleigh pram, lined with damask, from Eastern Townships. Length 47".
..................................$145

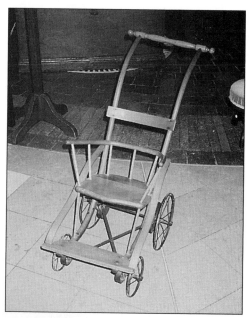

Ash and maple stroller with original iron wheels. By the Gendron Mfg. Co., Reed & Rattan Furniture, Toronto (original label). 1900-1910.
....$195

Unusual bass wood dual carriage, adjustable for wheels or sleigh. 1910-1920.
..........................$395

Child's

American origin baby carriage, with reversible handle and parasol, ca. 1840.
......................$1,395

All original wicker pram by the Heywood Carriage Co., ca. 1820.
.........................$1,450

Rare painted wooden baby carriage from Ontario, ca. 1820.
........................$1,250

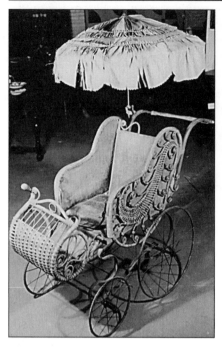

Top Left: Wicker carriage, all original including silk parasol. Wire wheels, rubber tires, foot brake. Early 1900s. Length 47".
....**$595**

Top Right: Wicker stroller. Wicker on metal frame, metal wheels with non-tip wheels at back, folding handle. Length 40".
.... **$170**

Bottom Left: Wicker carriage, metal and wood handle, rubber tires, adjustable hood. Length 47".
....**$225**

Bottom Right: Sleigh carriage, wicker and wood, adjustable hood, metal handle and runners, repainted red. Length 52".
....**$400**

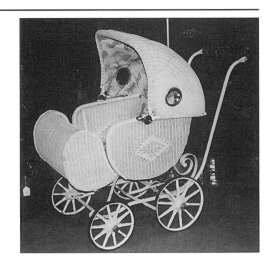

Wicker recliner baby carriage, wooden spoke wheels, lined hood with opera windows. Converts to go-cart, removable wheels. All original.
....**$475**

Victorian baby carriage, wicker body with removable and reversible hood, adjustable back rest, wood spokes and handles on metal frame, ca. 1890.
....**$425**

Eaton's wicker buggy with opera windows, ca. 1905. In excellent condition.
....**$450**

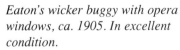

Carousel Horses

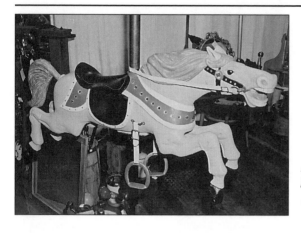

1926 C.W. Parker carousel
horse (excellent condition).
.....................................$5,000

Traveling carousel horse
(good condition), ca. 1895.
.................................$3,600

Security Device

Designed to be placed around
the wheel of the model "T"
Ford. This security auto-theft
device would make driving very
difficult and also if the car was
moved the sharp point would
indicate in the ground the
direction it had been taken.
.................No price available

The simplest toilet set consisted of a jug, basin and covered soap dish. Cheaper soap dishes were ridged inside to allow the soap to dry, whereas the more expensive ones had a removable liner. There was also a larger sponge bowl, often with separate perforated liner to allow air to circulate. A toothbrush holder and beaker was also part of the set, as was the chamber pot, which was kept in the bedside cabinet. A matching slop pail with wicker handle stood under the washstand ready to receive waste water.

The same china was often used on the dressing table. Covered pin boxes, powder bowls and candlesticks were set out, together with the stand for holding a lady's rings and a large tray for knick-knacks. In some of the larger sets, there were tall hatpin holders and toilet-water jugs. An object called a hair tidy matched the powder bowl, but is distinguishable by the circular hole in the lid, where the lady could dispose of loose hair from her brush and comb.

Jug, basin and soap dish. Unmarked. English Maypole scene with title "May Day" underneath. Brown trim on handle and around rim of jug. Height of jug 10½".
....$295 set

Losol ware jug and basin, "Shanghai" pattern, ca. 1912. Height of jug 13½". Diam. of bowl 16½".
....$495

Royal Doulton wash set. Two shades of green with yellow Art Nouveau pattern. Soap dish repaired. If all perfect
....$795

Jug and basin set, "Hilda" pattern by Wedgwood & Co., England in orange and gold. Note: Gold worn, and no lid to chamber pot.
....**$495**

Jug and basin set, "Hilda" pattern by Wedgwood & Co., England in blue and gold.
....**$825**

Washstand set, complete with covered chamber pot and slop pail. "Columbia" pattern by C & H Tunstall, England. Blue flowers on white ground with gold trim. Height of large water jug 11½". Height of slop pail (handle up) 16."
....**$1,250**

Four piece wash set by Furnival, Glasgow, Scotland. Black transfer maple leaf band with beaver in centre.
....**$1,750**

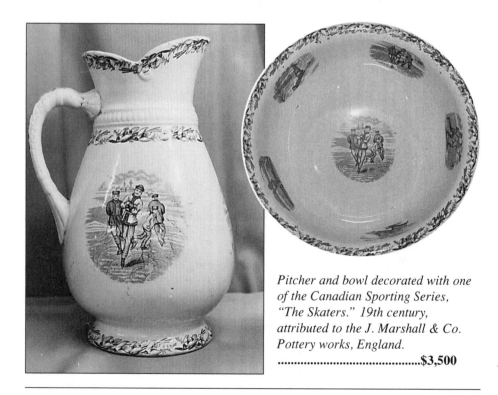

Pitcher and bowl decorated with one of the Canadian Sporting Series, "The Skaters." 19th century, attributed to the J. Marshall & Co. Pottery works, England.
....**$3,500**

Jug, basin and toothbrush holder. Green on white ground, with gold trim and flecking. Marked "Jersey, England." Height of jug 11¼".
..........................**$345 set**

Wash set complete with covered chamber pot, "Hampton" pattern by W.T.H. Smith, England, ca. 1899.
....**$850**

Wash set by W.H. Grindley & Co. Height of jug 9½".
....**$650**

Jug, basin and slop pail, "Cactus" pattern, by William Adderley Alsager & Co. Blue and gold outlined flowers on white ground with gold trim. Height of jug 10½". Diam. of bowl 16".
....**$450**

Jug and basin set. Deep maroon with gold trim. Height of large jug 12", small jug 8". Diam. of bowl 16". Five pieces.
....**$625**

Wash set, Royal Doulton "Merivale" pattern. Height of jug 12½". Diam. of bowl 16".
....**$750**

Jug and basin, flow blue "Popea" pattern by Grimwade, Staffordshire.
.................................$750

Jug and basin, pink and brown roses on blue and white ground. By Samuel Ford, Burslem, England. Height of jug 11½".
.....................................$225

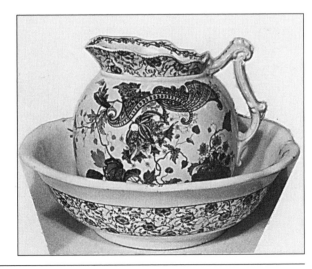

Jug and basin, floral decoration on white ground. Marked T & T Co., London.
.....................................$325

Washstand Sets

*Wash set, blue and white with gold trim by Alfred Meakin Ltd.,
England. Height of large jug 11¾". Diam. of bowl 15".*
....$675

*Wash set, "Fashoda" pattern by Dudson, Wilcox & Till Co., Hanley, England.
Pink floral on white ground. Height of large jug 13". Diam. of bowl 16".*
....$725

*Jug and basin in the "Tea Leaf"
pattern by Mellor, Taylor & Co.,
England. Height of jug 12½".
Diam. of bowl 14½".*
....$550

Jug and basin with covered soap dish. Blue on white ground. "Gloria" pattern by Dudson, Wilcox & Till Ltd., Hanley, England, ca. 1920.
....**$345**

Jug and basin, dark blue and white.
....**$335**

Jug and basin with slop pail, ca. 1850. Blue, purple and orange flowers, blue foliage on white ground. Height of large jug 11".
....**$450**

English wash set. Purple violets on white ground with black trim. Height of jug 11½".
......................................**$650**

Dresser set, pink glass, 1930s, English. Length of tray 12".
....**$145**

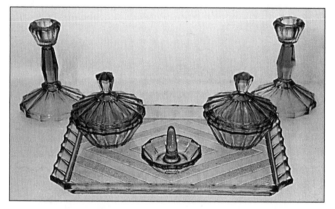

Dresser set, pink glass, 1940s, English. Tray 8" x 11".
....**$125**

Dresser set, pale green, 1940s, English. Length of tray 11".
....**$135**

Dresser set, Nippon, early 1900s. Scenic view with swans, heavily gilded (no tray).
....**$850**

Left: Barber bottle, amber with Mary Gregory type decoration and matching blown stopper. Ht. 8".
....**$475**

Right: Barber bottle, deep green, with Mary Gregory type decoration. Clear stopper not original. Ht. 7½".
....**$325**

Barber bottle, emerald green cut to clear. American. Ht. 6".
....**$145**

"Gibson Girl" shaving mug with flowers and gilding. Ht. 2¼". Diam. 3¼".
....$125

Lustre shaving mug, with "Brighton" (England) crest, gold trim round crest and rim. Ht. 4".
....$85

Unmarked. R.S. Prussia shaving mug with inset bevelled mirror.
...................................$275-$325

Skuttle shape shaving mugs. Left to Right:

German, early 1900s.
Transfer decorated, flowers
on white ground, gold trim.
Ht. 3½".
..................................$65

Lustre finish with garland
of flowers, gold trim.
Ht. 4".
..................................$145

German, early 1900s.
Transfer decorated, flowers
on white ground, gold trim.
Ht. 3¾".
..................................$75

Shaving mugs. Left to Right:

German, raised
bow with children
in rural scene,
impressed crest on
reverse. Ht. 3½".
....................$125

Gold trim on white
ground, inset
mirror. Ht. 3½".
....................$175

Heart shape, floral
bouquet, gold trim,
white ground.
Ht. 3½".
....................$135

Skuttle shape,
1890s. Applied blue
floral decoration on
front, blue trim.
Ht. 3½".
....................$125

Shaving mugs. Left to Right:

Pink, black and
green on white
ground, gold trim.
Ht. 2½".
....................$65

English, pink and
green on white
ground, pink lustre
trim. Ht. 2½".
....................$135

Austrian, hand
painted honeysuckle
and foliage on
white ground, gold
trim. Ht. 2".
....................$75

German, pink on
white ground, gold
trim. Ht. 2¼".
....................$115

Washstand Sets

INDEX

Index